Desktop Application
Complete Self-Assessment Guide

C000139561

The guidance in this Self-Assessment is base
best practices and standards in business process architecture, design
and quality management. The guidance is also based on the professional
judgment of the individual collaborators listed in the Acknowledgments.

Notice of rights

Trademarks

Table of Contents

About The Art of Service

The Art of Service, Business Process Architects since 2000, is dedicated to helping stakeholders achieve excellence.

Defining, designing, creating, and implementing a process to solve a stakeholders challenge or meet an objective is the most valuable role… In EVERY group, company, organization and department.

Unless you're talking a one-time, single-use project, there should be a process. Whether that process is managed and implemented by humans, AI, or a combination of the two, it needs to be designed by someone with a complex enough perspective to ask the right questions.

Someone capable of asking the right questions and step back and say, 'What are we really trying to accomplish here? And is there a different way to look at it?'

With The Art of Service's Standard Requirements Self-Assessments, we empower people who can do just that — whether their title is marketer, entrepreneur, manager, salesperson, consultant, Business Process Manager, executive assistant, IT Manager, CIO etc... —they are the people who rule the future. They are people who watch the process as it happens, and ask the right questions to make the process work better.

Contact us when you need any support with this Self-Assessment and any help with templates, blue-prints and examples of standard documents you might need:

http://theartofservice.com
service@theartofservice.com

Included Resources - how to access

Included with your purchase of the book is the Desktop

Application Self-Assessment Spreadsheet Dashboard which contains all questions and Self-Assessment areas and auto-generates insights, graphs, and project RACI planning - all with examples to get you started right away.

How? Simply send an email to
access@theartofservice.com
with this books' title in the subject to get the Desktop Application Self Assessment Tool right away.

You will receive the following contents with New and Updated specific criteria:

- The latest quick edition of the book in PDF

- The latest complete edition of the book in PDF, which criteria correspond to the criteria in...

- The Self-Assessment Excel Dashboard, and...

- Example pre-filled Self-Assessment Excel Dashboard to get familiar with results generation

- In-depth specific Checklists covering the topic

- Project management checklists and templates to assist with implementation

INCLUDES LIFETIME SELF ASSESSMENT UPDATES

Every self assessment comes with Lifetime Updates and Lifetime Free Updated Books. Lifetime Updates is an industry-first feature which allows you to receive verified self assessment updates, ensuring you always have the most accurate information at your fingertips.

Get it now- you will be glad you did - do it now, before you forget.

Send an email to **access@theartofservice.com** with this books' title in the subject to get the Desktop Application Self Assessment Tool right away.

Purpose of this Self-Assessment

This Self-Assessment has been developed to improve understanding of the requirements and elements of Desktop Application, based on best practices and standards in business process architecture, design and quality management.

It is designed to allow for a rapid Self-Assessment to determine how closely existing management practices and procedures correspond to the elements of the Self-Assessment.

The criteria of requirements and elements of Desktop Application have been rephrased in the format of a Self-Assessment questionnaire, with a seven-criterion scoring system, as explained in this document.

In this format, even with limited background knowledge of Desktop Application, a manager can quickly review existing operations to determine how they measure up to the standards. This in turn can serve as the starting point of a 'gap analysis' to identify management tools or system elements that might usefully be implemented in the organization to help improve overall performance.

How to use the Self-Assessment

On the following pages are a series of questions to identify to what extent your Desktop Application initiative is complete in comparison to the requirements set in standards.

To facilitate answering the questions, there is a space in front of each question to enter a score on a scale of '1' to '5'.

1 Strongly Disagree

2 Disagree

3 Neutral

4 Agree

5 Strongly Agree

Read the question and rate it with the following in front of mind:

'In my belief,
the answer to this question is clearly defined'.

There are two ways in which you can choose to interpret this statement;
1. how aware are you that the answer to the question is clearly defined
2. for more in-depth analysis you can choose to gather evidence and confirm the answer to the question. This obviously will take more time, most Self-Assessment users opt for the first way to interpret the question and dig deeper later on based on the outcome of the overall Self-Assessment.

A score of '1' would mean that the answer is not clear at all, where a '5' would mean the answer is crystal clear and defined. Leave emtpy when the question is not applicable or you don't want to answer it, you can skip it without affecting your score. Write your score in the space provided.

After you have responded to all the appropriate statements in each section, compute your average score for that section, using the formula provided, and round to the nearest tenth. Then transfer to the corresponding spoke in the Desktop Application Scorecard on the second next page of the Self-Assessment.

Your completed Desktop Application Scorecard will give you a clear presentation of which Desktop Application areas need attention.

Desktop Application
Scorecard Example

Example of how the finalized Scorecard can look like:

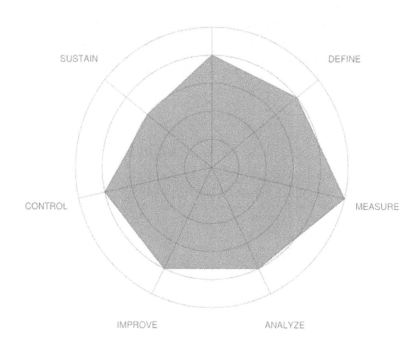

Desktop Application Scorecard

Your Scores:

BEGINNING OF THE SELF-ASSESSMENT:

CRITERION #1: RECOGNIZE

INTENT: Be aware of the need for change. Recognize that there is an unfavorable variation, problem or symptom.

In my belief, the answer to this question is clearly defined:

5 Strongly Agree

4 Agree

3 Neutral

2 Disagree

1 Strongly Disagree

1. What are the stakeholder objectives to be achieved with desktop application?
<--- Score

2. Do you have/need 24-hour access to key personnel?
<--- Score

3. Which needs are not included or involved?
<--- Score

4. Are there recognized desktop application problems?
<--- Score

5. Do you recognize desktop application achievements?
<--- Score

6. What are your needs in relation to desktop application skills, labor, equipment, and markets?
<--- Score

7. Who defines the rules in relation to any given issue?
<--- Score

8. What are the clients issues and concerns?
<--- Score

9. What else needs to be measured?
<--- Score

10. How much are sponsors, customers, partners, stakeholders involved in desktop application? In other words, what are the risks, if desktop application does not deliver successfully?
<--- Score

11. What problems are you facing and how do you consider desktop application will circumvent those obstacles?
<--- Score

12. Did you miss any major desktop application issues?
<--- Score

13. What activities does the governance board need to consider?
<--- Score

14. To what extent would your organization benefit from being recognized as a award recipient?
<--- Score

15. What should be considered when identifying available resources, constraints, and deadlines?
<--- Score

16. Are there desktop application problems defined?
<--- Score

17. What desktop application coordination do you need?
<--- Score

18. What vendors make products that address the desktop application needs?
<--- Score

19. Who else hopes to benefit from it?
<--- Score

20. How are training requirements identified?
<--- Score

21. What tools and technologies are needed for a custom desktop application project?
<--- Score

22. What is the problem or issue?
<--- Score

23. Why the need?
<--- Score

24. Will new equipment/products be required to facilitate desktop application delivery, for example is new software needed?
<--- Score

25. Is the quality assurance team identified?
<--- Score

26. What is the extent or complexity of the desktop application problem?
<--- Score

27. For your desktop application project, identify and describe the business environment, is there more than one layer to the business environment?
<--- Score

28. As a sponsor, customer or management, how important is it to meet goals, objectives?
<--- Score

29. What information do users need?
<--- Score

30. How are the desktop application's objectives aligned to the group's overall stakeholder strategy?
<--- Score

31. What does desktop application success mean to the stakeholders?
<--- Score

32. When a desktop application manager recognizes a problem, what options are available?
<--- Score

33. Are there regulatory / compliance issues?
<--- Score

34. Have you identified your desktop application key performance indicators?
<--- Score

35. How do you take a forward-looking perspective in identifying desktop application research related to market response and models?
<--- Score

36. What do you need to start doing?
<--- Score

37. What is the desktop application problem definition? What do you need to resolve?
<--- Score

38. Who should resolve the desktop application issues?
<--- Score

39. Does the problem have ethical dimensions?
<--- Score

40. What extra resources will you need?
<--- Score

41. Will desktop application deliverables need to be tested and, if so, by whom?
<--- Score

42. How do you recognize an objection?
<--- Score

43. Are problem definition and motivation clearly presented?
<--- Score

44. What situation(s) led to this desktop application Self Assessment?
<--- Score

45. Is the need for organizational change recognized?
<--- Score

46. What do employees need in the short term?
<--- Score

47. Is it clear when you think of the day ahead of you what activities and tasks you need to complete?
<--- Score

48. What are the expected benefits of desktop application to the stakeholder?
<--- Score

49. To what extent does each concerned units management team recognize desktop application as an effective investment?
<--- Score

50. Are there any specific expectations or concerns about the desktop application team, desktop application itself?
<--- Score

51. How do you assess your desktop application workforce capability and capacity needs, including skills, competencies, and staffing levels?
<--- Score

52. Which information does the desktop application business case need to include?
<--- Score

53. Who needs to know?
<--- Score

54. What needs to stay?
<--- Score

55. Who are your key stakeholders who need to sign off?
<--- Score

56. Do you need different information or graphics?
<--- Score

57. Think about the people you identified for your desktop application project and the project responsibilities you would assign to them, what kind of training do you think they would need to perform these responsibilities effectively?
<--- Score

58. How do you identify the kinds of information that you will need?
<--- Score

59. Are you dealing with any of the same issues today as yesterday? What can you do about this?
<--- Score

60. Consider your own desktop application project, what types of organizational problems do you think might be causing or affecting your problem, based on the work done so far?
<--- Score

61. Looking at each person individually – does every one have the qualities which are needed to work in this group?
<--- Score

62. What are the timeframes required to resolve each of the issues/problems?
<--- Score

63. Why is this needed?
<--- Score

64. What creative shifts do you need to take?
<--- Score

65. What training and capacity building actions are needed to implement proposed reforms?
<--- Score

66. Do you need to avoid or amend any desktop application activities?
<--- Score

67. Does your organization need more desktop application education?
<--- Score

68. What are the minority interests and what amount of minority interests can be recognized?

<--- Score

69. What is the problem and/or vulnerability?
<--- Score

70. Who needs to know about desktop application?
<--- Score

71. What desktop application events should you attend?
<--- Score

72. What desktop application capabilities do you need?
<--- Score

73. What needs to be done?
<--- Score

74. Is it needed?
<--- Score

75. Can management personnel recognize the monetary benefit of desktop application?
<--- Score

76. How does it fit into your organizational needs and tasks?
<--- Score

77. Does desktop application create potential expectations in other areas that need to be recognized and considered?
<--- Score

78. Which issues are too important to ignore?

<--- Score

79. What prevents you from making the changes you know will make you a more effective desktop application leader?
<--- Score

80. Who needs budgets?
<--- Score

81. What would happen if desktop application weren't done?
<--- Score

82. Are losses recognized in a timely manner?
<--- Score

83. Would you recognize a threat from the inside?
<--- Score

84. Are employees recognized or rewarded for performance that demonstrates the highest levels of integrity?
<--- Score

85. Are there any revenue recognition issues?
<--- Score

86. Will a response program recognize when a crisis occurs and provide some level of response?
<--- Score

87. Where do you need to exercise leadership?
<--- Score

88. What is the smallest subset of the problem you

can usefully solve?
<--- Score

89. Who needs what information?
<--- Score

90. What desktop application problem should be solved?
<--- Score

91. Will it solve real problems?
<--- Score

92. How do you recognize an desktop application objection?
<--- Score

93. Are employees recognized for desired behaviors?
<--- Score

94. How do you identify subcontractor relationships?
<--- Score

95. What resources or support might you need?
<--- Score

96. Whom do you really need or want to serve?
<--- Score

97. How are you going to measure success?
<--- Score

Add up total points for this section:
_ _ _ _ _ = Total points for this section

Divided by: _ _ _ _ _ _ (number of

statements answered) = _ _ _ _ _ _
Average score for this section

Transfer your score to the desktop
application Index at the beginning of
the Self-Assessment.

CRITERION #2: DEFINE:

INTENT: Formulate the stakeholder problem. Define the problem, needs and objectives.

In my belief, the answer to this question is clearly defined:

5 Strongly Agree

4 Agree

3 Neutral

2 Disagree

1 Strongly Disagree

1. What are the Roles and Responsibilities for each team member and its leadership? Where is this documented?
<--- Score

2. How do you gather requirements?
<--- Score

3. What are the desktop application tasks and

definitions?

<--- Score

4. How have you defined all desktop application requirements first?

<--- Score

5. What customer feedback methods were used to solicit their input?

<--- Score

6. How often are the team meetings?

<--- Score

7. Will team members regularly document their desktop application work?

<--- Score

8. Scope of sensitive information?

<--- Score

9. How does the desktop application manager ensure against scope creep?

<--- Score

10. Are improvement team members fully trained on desktop application?

<--- Score

11. If substitutes have been appointed, have they been briefed on the desktop application goals and received regular communications as to the progress to date?

<--- Score

12. Is there a completed, verified, and validated high-

level 'as is' (not 'should be' or 'could be') stakeholder process map?
<--- Score

13. When are meeting minutes sent out? Who is on the distribution list?
<--- Score

14. Are all requirements met?
<--- Score

15. Are customers identified and high impact areas defined?
<--- Score

16. What is the definition of desktop application excellence?
<--- Score

17. What is the scope of the desktop application effort?
<--- Score

18. Are required metrics defined, what are they?
<--- Score

19. Who is gathering desktop application information?
<--- Score

20. What are the compelling stakeholder reasons for embarking on desktop application?
<--- Score

21. Is there regularly 100% attendance at the team meetings? If not, have appointed substitutes attended to preserve cross-functionality and full

representation?
<--- Score

22. Is it clearly defined in and to your organization what you do?
<--- Score

23. Has the desktop application work been fairly and/or equitably divided and delegated among team members who are qualified and capable to perform the work? Has everyone contributed?
<--- Score

24. Are accountability and ownership for desktop application clearly defined?
<--- Score

25. What are the rough order estimates on cost savings/opportunities that desktop application brings?
<--- Score

26. What are (control) requirements for desktop application Information?
<--- Score

27. Where can you gather more information?
<--- Score

28. How is the team tracking and documenting its work?
<--- Score

29. What baselines are required to be defined and managed?
<--- Score

30. Are stakeholder processes mapped?
<--- Score

31. Has your scope been defined?
<--- Score

32. What is the definition of success?
<--- Score

33. Have all of the relationships been defined properly?
<--- Score

34. Who are the desktop application improvement team members, including Management Leads and Coaches?
<--- Score

35. Is there a critical path to deliver desktop application results?
<--- Score

36. Is there any additional desktop application definition of success?
<--- Score

37. What is the scope of the desktop application work?
<--- Score

38. Are customer(s) identified and segmented according to their different needs and requirements?
<--- Score

39. Is the current 'as is' process being followed? If not,

what are the discrepancies?
<--- Score

40. When is the estimated completion date?
<--- Score

41. Is the team formed and are team leaders (Coaches and Management Leads) assigned?
<--- Score

42. Is the scope of desktop application defined?
<--- Score

43. How will variation in the actual durations of each activity be dealt with to ensure that the expected desktop application results are met?
<--- Score

44. Has the improvement team collected the 'voice of the customer' (obtained feedback – qualitative and quantitative)?
<--- Score

45. Is data collected and displayed to better understand customer(s) critical needs and requirements.
<--- Score

46. How are consistent desktop application definitions important?
<--- Score

47. Is there a clear desktop application case definition?
<--- Score

48. Has a team charter been developed and communicated?
<--- Score

49. Is desktop application currently on schedule according to the plan?
<--- Score

50. How do you manage scope?
<--- Score

51. Are audit criteria, scope, frequency and methods defined?
<--- Score

52. What sources do you use to gather information for a desktop application study?
<--- Score

53. Are there any constraints known that bear on the ability to perform desktop application work? How is the team addressing them?
<--- Score

54. Is the work to date meeting requirements?
<--- Score

55. What is the worst case scenario?
<--- Score

56. Is special desktop application user knowledge required?
<--- Score

57. Has the direction changed at all during the course of desktop application? If so, when did it change and

why?
<--- Score

58. What critical content must be communicated –
who, what, when, where, and how?
<--- Score

59. What are the dynamics of the communication
plan?
<--- Score

60. How do you gather desktop application
requirements?
<--- Score

61. What are the tasks and definitions?
<--- Score

62. How do you manage changes in desktop
application requirements?
<--- Score

63. Do you all define desktop application in the same
way?
<--- Score

64. Has everyone on the team, including the team
leaders, been properly trained?
<--- Score

65. What are the desktop application use cases?
<--- Score

66. What was the context?
<--- Score

67. Are the desktop application requirements complete?
<--- Score

68. What desktop application requirements should be gathered?
<--- Score

69. Have the customer needs been translated into specific, measurable requirements? How?
<--- Score

70. What are the core elements of the desktop application business case?
<--- Score

71. Is the desktop application scope manageable?
<--- Score

72. Who approved the desktop application scope?
<--- Score

73. Is the desktop application scope complete and appropriately sized?
<--- Score

74. Has a high-level 'as is' process map been completed, verified and validated?
<--- Score

75. Are resources adequate for the scope?
<--- Score

76. Who defines (or who defined) the rules and roles?
<--- Score

77. What key stakeholder process output measure(s) does desktop application leverage and how?
<--- Score

78. The political context: who holds power?
<--- Score

79. Is there a desktop application management charter, including stakeholder case, problem and goal statements, scope, milestones, roles and responsibilities, communication plan?
<--- Score

80. How do you catch desktop application definition inconsistencies?
<--- Score

81. What knowledge or experience is required?
<--- Score

82. What are the record-keeping requirements of desktop application activities?
<--- Score

83. Are different versions of process maps needed to account for the different types of inputs?
<--- Score

84. What information do you gather?
<--- Score

85. Has anyone else (internal or external to the group) attempted to solve this problem or a similar one before? If so, what knowledge can be leveraged from these previous efforts?
<--- Score

86. Will a desktop application production readiness review be required?
<--- Score

87. What are the requirements for audit information?
<--- Score

88. Are approval levels defined for contracts and supplements to contracts?
<--- Score

89. How did the desktop application manager receive input to the development of a desktop application improvement plan and the estimated completion dates/times of each activity?
<--- Score

90. What specifically is the problem? Where does it occur? When does it occur? What is its extent?
<--- Score

91. What gets examined?
<--- Score

92. Is the improvement team aware of the different versions of a process: what they think it is vs. what it actually is vs. what it should be vs. what it could be?
<--- Score

93. Does the team have regular meetings?
<--- Score

94. Is there a completed SIPOC representation, describing the Suppliers, Inputs, Process, Outputs, and Customers?

<--- Score

95. How do you gather the stories?
<--- Score

96. What information should you gather?
<--- Score

97. What are the boundaries of the scope? What is in bounds and what is not? What is the start point? What is the stop point?
<--- Score

98. How do you keep key subject matter experts in the loop?
<--- Score

99. Is scope creep really all bad news?
<--- Score

100. Do you have a desktop application success story or case study ready to tell and share?
<--- Score

101. Is the team sponsored by a champion or stakeholder leader?
<--- Score

102. Are roles and responsibilities formally defined?
<--- Score

103. What desktop application services do you require?
<--- Score

104. Are task requirements clearly defined?

<--- Score

105. When is/was the desktop application start date?
<--- Score

106. Has/have the customer(s) been identified?
<--- Score

107. What is the context?
<--- Score

108. Why are you doing desktop application and what is the scope?
<--- Score

109. Do the problem and goal statements meet the SMART criteria (specific, measurable, attainable, relevant, and time-bound)?
<--- Score

110. How can the value of desktop application be defined?
<--- Score

111. What is in the scope and what is not in scope?
<--- Score

112. Has a desktop application requirement not been met?
<--- Score

113. Is the team equipped with available and reliable resources?
<--- Score

114. What intelligence can you gather?

<--- Score

115. What is in scope?
<--- Score

116. What scope to assess?
<--- Score

117. What constraints exist that might impact the team?
<--- Score

118. In what way can you redefine the criteria of choice clients have in your category in your favor?
<--- Score

119. Has a project plan, Gantt chart, or similar been developed/completed?
<--- Score

120. Are team charters developed?
<--- Score

121. What sort of initial information to gather?
<--- Score

122. Do you have organizational privacy requirements?
<--- Score

123. Are there different segments of customers?
<--- Score

124. Is desktop application linked to key stakeholder goals and objectives?
<--- Score

125. What is out of scope?
<--- Score

126. Will team members perform desktop application work when assigned and in a timely fashion?
<--- Score

127. How was the 'as is' process map developed, reviewed, verified and validated?
<--- Score

128. What is a worst-case scenario for losses?
<--- Score

129. How and when will the baselines be defined?
<--- Score

130. Have all basic functions of desktop application been defined?
<--- Score

131. How do you hand over desktop application context?
<--- Score

132. How will the desktop application team and the group measure complete success of desktop application?
<--- Score

133. What defines best in class?
<--- Score

134. What would be the goal or target for a desktop application's improvement team?

<--- Score

135. What is the scope of desktop application?
<--- Score

136. Is full participation by members in regularly held team meetings guaranteed?
<--- Score

137. Is the team adequately staffed with the desired cross-functionality? If not, what additional resources are available to the team?
<--- Score

138. Does the scope remain the same?
<--- Score

139. How do you manage unclear desktop application requirements?
<--- Score

Add up total points for this section:
_ _ _ _ _ = Total points for this section

Divided by: _ _ _ _ _ _ (number of statements answered) = _ _ _ _ _ _ Average score for this section

Transfer your score to the desktop application Index at the beginning of the Self-Assessment.

CRITERION #3: MEASURE:

INTENT: Gather the correct data. Measure the current performance and evolution of the situation.

In my belief, the answer to this question is clearly defined:

5 Strongly Agree

4 Agree

3 Neutral

2 Disagree

1 Strongly Disagree

1. How do your measurements capture actionable desktop application information for use in exceeding your customers expectations and securing your customers engagement?
<--- Score

2. What is the total fixed cost?
<--- Score

3. Among the desktop application product and service cost to be estimated, which is considered hardest to estimate?
<--- Score

4. What measurements are being captured?
<--- Score

5. How do you prevent mis-estimating cost?
<--- Score

6. Are you able to realize any cost savings?
<--- Score

7. How will you measure your desktop application effectiveness?
<--- Score

8. What methods are feasible and acceptable to estimate the impact of reforms?
<--- Score

9. Are there measurements based on task performance?
<--- Score

10. Are desktop application vulnerabilities categorized and prioritized?
<--- Score

11. What do people want to verify?
<--- Score

12. What is the cause of any desktop application gaps?
<--- Score

13. How do you verify performance?
<--- Score

14. What causes investor action?
<--- Score

15. Are actual costs in line with budgeted costs?
<--- Score

16. Is the solution cost-effective?
<--- Score

17. Are you aware of what could cause a problem?
<--- Score

18. What are the desktop application investment costs?
<--- Score

19. Does a desktop application quantification method exist?
<--- Score

20. How will your organization measure success?
<--- Score

21. How will effects be measured?
<--- Score

22. What relevant entities could be measured?
<--- Score

23. What disadvantage does this cause for the user?
<--- Score

24. Have you included everything in your desktop

application cost models?
<--- Score

25. At what cost?
<--- Score

26. What are the strategic priorities for this year?
<--- Score

27. Which measures and indicators matter?
<--- Score

28. How do you measure variability?
<--- Score

29. What are allowable costs?
<--- Score

30. How do you measure efficient delivery of desktop application services?
<--- Score

31. What is an unallowable cost?
<--- Score

32. What is the root cause(s) of the problem?
<--- Score

33. What causes innovation to fail or succeed in your organization?
<--- Score

34. What do you measure and why?
<--- Score

35. Why do you expend time and effort to implement

measurement, for whom?
<--- Score

36. Are the desktop application benefits worth its costs?
<--- Score

37. Do you effectively measure and reward individual and team performance?
<--- Score

38. What evidence is there and what is measured?
<--- Score

39. Was a business case (cost/benefit) developed?
<--- Score

40. What are your primary costs, revenues, assets?
<--- Score

41. What potential environmental factors impact the desktop application effort?
<--- Score

42. What is the desktop application business impact?
<--- Score

43. What are the estimated costs of proposed changes?
<--- Score

44. What tests verify requirements?
<--- Score

45. What could cause you to change course?
<--- Score

46. What can be used to verify compliance?
<--- Score

47. How are costs allocated?
<--- Score

48. What happens if cost savings do not materialize?
<--- Score

49. How do you control the overall costs of your work processes?
<--- Score

50. What is the total cost related to deploying desktop application, including any consulting or professional services?
<--- Score

51. Do you have an issue in getting priority?
<--- Score

52. What are your operating costs?
<--- Score

53. What users will be impacted?
<--- Score

54. What are the costs?
<--- Score

55. How do you verify the desktop application requirements quality?
<--- Score

56. Have you made assumptions about the shape of

the future, particularly its impact on your customers and competitors?

<--- Score

57. How do you quantify and qualify impacts?

<--- Score

58. When are costs are incurred?

<--- Score

59. Do you have any cost desktop application limitation requirements?

<--- Score

60. What are the operational costs after desktop application deployment?

<--- Score

61. Do the benefits outweigh the costs?

<--- Score

62. What are the current costs of the desktop application process?

<--- Score

63. Which costs should be taken into account?

<--- Score

64. When a disaster occurs, who gets priority?

<--- Score

65. Is it possible to estimate the impact of unanticipated complexity such as wrong or failed assumptions, feedback, etcetera on proposed reforms?

<--- Score

66. Are you taking your company in the direction of better and revenue or cheaper and cost?
<--- Score

67. What does a Test Case verify?
<--- Score

68. What causes extra work or rework?
<--- Score

69. How are measurements made?
<--- Score

70. What causes mismanagement?
<--- Score

71. Will desktop application have an impact on current business continuity, disaster recovery processes and/or infrastructure?
<--- Score

72. What are the types and number of measures to use?
<--- Score

73. How can you reduce costs?
<--- Score

74. Are the units of measure consistent?
<--- Score

75. What are your customers expectations and measures?
<--- Score

76. Are the measurements objective?
<--- Score

77. Where is it measured?
<--- Score

78. Are supply costs steady or fluctuating?
<--- Score

79. How do you verify your resources?
<--- Score

80. What would it cost to replace your technology?
<--- Score

81. How will measures be used to manage and adapt?
<--- Score

82. What are the costs and benefits?
<--- Score

83. How do you aggregate measures across priorities?
<--- Score

84. How much does it cost?
<--- Score

85. How will success or failure be measured?
<--- Score

86. What are your key desktop application organizational performance measures, including key short and longer-term financial measures?
<--- Score

87. How will costs be allocated?

<--- Score

88. Does the desktop application task fit the client's priorities?
<--- Score

89. How is progress measured?
<--- Score

90. What are you verifying?
<--- Score

91. Do you aggressively reward and promote the people who have the biggest impact on creating excellent desktop application services/products?
<--- Score

92. Where is the cost?
<--- Score

93. How is performance measured?
<--- Score

94. Why do the measurements/indicators matter?
<--- Score

95. How can a desktop application test verify your ideas or assumptions?
<--- Score

96. How long to keep data and how to manage retention costs?
<--- Score

97. Where can you go to verify the info?
<--- Score

98. Are there competing desktop application priorities?
<--- Score

99. How do you measure lifecycle phases?
<--- Score

100. What are hidden desktop application quality costs?
<--- Score

101. Who pays the cost?
<--- Score

102. Are there any easy-to-implement alternatives to desktop application? Sometimes other solutions are available that do not require the cost implications of a full-blown project?
<--- Score

103. Is there an opportunity to verify requirements?
<--- Score

104. How do you measure success?
<--- Score

105. How can you manage cost down?
<--- Score

106. What harm might be caused?
<--- Score

107. What drives O&M cost?
<--- Score

108. What is the cost of rework?
<--- Score

109. What are the costs of delaying desktop application action?
<--- Score

110. How can you reduce the costs of obtaining inputs?
<--- Score

111. How do you verify and develop ideas and innovations?
<--- Score

112. Does management have the right priorities among projects?
<--- Score

113. What are the desktop application key cost drivers?
<--- Score

114. What details are required of the desktop application cost structure?
<--- Score

115. How is the value delivered by desktop application being measured?
<--- Score

116. How sensitive must the desktop application strategy be to cost?
<--- Score

117. How do you verify the authenticity of the data

and information used?
<--- Score

118. Has a cost center been established?
<--- Score

119. How will you measure success?
<--- Score

120. Is the cost worth the desktop application effort ?
<--- Score

121. What could cause delays in the schedule?
<--- Score

122. What does losing customers cost your organization?
<--- Score

123. How frequently do you track desktop application measures?
<--- Score

124. How can you measure desktop application in a systematic way?
<--- Score

125. What are the uncertainties surrounding estimates of impact?
<--- Score

126. Do you have a flow diagram of what happens?
<--- Score

127. What measurements are possible, practicable and meaningful?

<--- Score

128. What would be a real cause for concern?
<--- Score

129. How to cause the change?
<--- Score

130. What are the costs of reform?
<--- Score

131. What does your operating model cost?
<--- Score

132. Did you tackle the cause or the symptom?
<--- Score

133. How can you measure the performance?
<--- Score

134. Which desktop application impacts are significant?
<--- Score

135. When should you bother with diagrams?
<--- Score

136. What is your desktop application quality cost segregation study?
<--- Score

137. Are indirect costs charged to the desktop application program?
<--- Score

Add up total points for this section:

_____ = Total points for this section

Divided by: _____ (number of
statements answered) = _____
Average score for this section

Transfer your score to the desktop
application Index at the beginning of
the Self-Assessment.

CRITERION #4: ANALYZE:

INTENT: Analyze causes, assumptions and hypotheses.

In my belief, the answer to this question is clearly defined:

5 Strongly Agree

4 Agree

3 Neutral

2 Disagree

1 Strongly Disagree

1. Has data output been validated?
<--- Score

2. Is the final output clearly identified?
<--- Score

3. What training and qualifications will you need?
<--- Score

4. How are outputs preserved and protected?

<--- Score

5. Who qualifies to gain access to data?
<--- Score

6. Have you defined which data is gathered how?
<--- Score

7. What are your best practices for minimizing desktop application project risk, while demonstrating incremental value and quick wins throughout the desktop application project lifecycle?
<--- Score

8. Do several people in different organizational units assist with the desktop application process?
<--- Score

9. Is there a strict change management process?
<--- Score

10. How do mission and objectives affect the desktop application processes of your organization?
<--- Score

11. Is pre-qualification of suppliers carried out?
<--- Score

12. How is the desktop application Value Stream Mapping managed?
<--- Score

13. Do you understand your management processes today?
<--- Score

14. What internal processes need improvement?
<--- Score

15. How will corresponding data be collected?
<--- Score

16. What resources go in to get the desired output?
<--- Score

17. How will the desktop application data be captured?
<--- Score

18. What did the team gain from developing a sub-process map?
<--- Score

19. Do your employees have the opportunity to do what they do best everyday?
<--- Score

20. What conclusions were drawn from the team's data collection and analysis? How did the team reach these conclusions?
<--- Score

21. What are your key performance measures or indicators and in-process measures for the control and improvement of your desktop application processes?
<--- Score

22. Is the gap/opportunity displayed and communicated in financial terms?
<--- Score

23. What desktop application data do you gather or use now?
<--- Score

24. Who will gather what data?
<--- Score

25. Is the desktop application process severely broken such that a re-design is necessary?
<--- Score

26. Have any additional benefits been identified that will result from closing all or most of the gaps?
<--- Score

27. Is data and process analysis, root cause analysis and quantifying the gap/opportunity in place?
<--- Score

28. What are the disruptive desktop application technologies that enable your organization to radically change your business processes?
<--- Score

29. Who gets your output?
<--- Score

30. Which desktop application data should be retained?
<--- Score

31. How often will data be collected for measures?
<--- Score

32. What is the Value Stream Mapping?
<--- Score

33. How do your work systems and key work processes relate to and capitalize on your core competencies?
<--- Score

34. Where can you get qualified talent today?
<--- Score

35. Were Pareto charts (or similar) used to portray the 'heavy hitters' (or key sources of variation)?
<--- Score

36. Record-keeping requirements flow from the records needed as inputs, outputs, controls and for transformation of a desktop application process, are the records needed as inputs to the desktop application process available?
<--- Score

37. What process should you select for improvement?
<--- Score

38. What qualifications are necessary?
<--- Score

39. What were the financial benefits resulting from any 'ground fruit or low-hanging fruit' (quick fixes)?
<--- Score

40. Do you, as a leader, bounce back quickly from setbacks?
<--- Score

41. What qualifications and skills do you need?
<--- Score

42. Do you have the authority to produce the output?
<--- Score

43. Do quality systems drive continuous improvement?
<--- Score

44. What are the necessary qualifications?
<--- Score

45. How is desktop application data gathered?
<--- Score

46. Did any value-added analysis or 'lean thinking' take place to identify some of the gaps shown on the 'as is' process map?
<--- Score

47. What methods do you use to gather desktop application data?
<--- Score

48. What desktop application data will be collected?
<--- Score

49. Do your contracts/agreements contain data security obligations?
<--- Score

50. How difficult is it to qualify what desktop application ROI is?
<--- Score

51. What tools were used to generate the list of possible causes?

<--- Score

52. What, related to, desktop application processes does your organization outsource?
<--- Score

53. What is the output?
<--- Score

54. What are the desktop application business drivers?
<--- Score

55. Think about the functions involved in your desktop application project, what processes flow from these functions?
<--- Score

56. How do you identify specific desktop application investment opportunities and emerging trends?
<--- Score

57. When should a process be art not science?
<--- Score

58. Can you add value to the current desktop application decision-making process (largely qualitative) by incorporating uncertainty modeling (more quantitative)?
<--- Score

59. How do you promote understanding that opportunity for improvement is not criticism of the status quo, or the people who created the status quo?
<--- Score

60. What are your desktop application processes?

<--- Score

61. Think about some of the processes you undertake within your organization, which do you own?
<--- Score

62. What are the processes for audit reporting and management?
<--- Score

63. Who owns what data?
<--- Score

64. What systems/processes must you excel at?
<--- Score

65. How do you ensure that the desktop application opportunity is realistic?
<--- Score

66. Who will facilitate the team and process?
<--- Score

67. An organizationally feasible system request is one that considers the mission, goals and objectives of the organization, key questions are: is the desktop application solution request practical and will it solve a problem or take advantage of an opportunity to achieve company goals?
<--- Score

68. Did any additional data need to be collected?
<--- Score

69. What is your organizations system for selecting qualified vendors?

<--- Score

70. What will drive desktop application change?
<--- Score

71. What is the oversight process?
<--- Score

72. Was a detailed process map created to amplify critical steps of the 'as is' stakeholder process?
<--- Score

73. Do your leaders quickly bounce back from setbacks?
<--- Score

74. Are your outputs consistent?
<--- Score

75. What process improvements will be needed?
<--- Score

76. What are your current levels and trends in key desktop application measures or indicators of product and process performance that are important to and directly serve your customers?
<--- Score

77. How is data used for program management and improvement?
<--- Score

78. What are the revised rough estimates of the financial savings/opportunity for desktop application improvements?
<--- Score

79. How does the organization define, manage, and improve its desktop application processes?
<--- Score

80. What is the desktop application Driver?
<--- Score

81. What are your outputs?
<--- Score

82. Who is involved with workflow mapping?
<--- Score

83. Was a cause-and-effect diagram used to explore the different types of causes (or sources of variation)?
<--- Score

84. Are all staff in core desktop application subjects Highly Qualified?
<--- Score

85. What kind of crime could a potential new hire have committed that would not only not disqualify him/her from being hired by your organization, but would actually indicate that he/she might be a particularly good fit?
<--- Score

86. A compounding model resolution with available relevant data can often provide insight towards a solution methodology; which desktop application models, tools and techniques are necessary?
<--- Score

87. How do you use desktop application data and

information to support organizational decision making and innovation?

<--- Score

88. How many input/output points does it require?

<--- Score

89. What does the data say about the performance of the stakeholder process?

<--- Score

90. How is the way you as the leader think and process information affecting your organizational culture?

<--- Score

91. Have the problem and goal statements been updated to reflect the additional knowledge gained from the analyze phase?

<--- Score

92. Is there an established change management process?

<--- Score

93. Should you invest in industry-recognized qualifications?

<--- Score

94. Are desktop application changes recognized early enough to be approved through the regular process?

<--- Score

95. Were there any improvement opportunities identified from the process analysis?

<--- Score

96. What is your organizations process which leads to recognition of value generation?
<--- Score

97. What data do you need to collect?
<--- Score

98. What controls do you have in place to protect data?
<--- Score

99. What desktop application data should be managed?
<--- Score

100. Is there any way to speed up the process?
<--- Score

101. How will the change process be managed?
<--- Score

102. What desktop application metrics are outputs of the process?
<--- Score

103. What do you need to qualify?
<--- Score

104. What tools were used to narrow the list of possible causes?
<--- Score

105. Are all team members qualified for all tasks?
<--- Score

106. What are your current levels and trends in key

measures or indicators of desktop application product and process performance that are important to and directly serve your customers? How do these results compare with the performance of your competitors and other organizations with similar offerings?
<--- Score

107. What other organizational variables, such as reward systems or communication systems, affect the performance of this desktop application process?
<--- Score

108. Is the performance gap determined?
<--- Score

109. Were any designed experiments used to generate additional insight into the data analysis?
<--- Score

110. How has the desktop application data been gathered?
<--- Score

111. What desktop application data should be collected?
<--- Score

112. What other jobs or tasks affect the performance of the steps in the desktop application process?
<--- Score

113. Are gaps between current performance and the goal performance identified?
<--- Score

114. What qualifies as competition?

<--- Score

115. How can risk management be tied procedurally to process elements?
<--- Score

116. What successful thing are you doing today that may be blinding you to new growth opportunities?
<--- Score

117. What quality tools were used to get through the analyze phase?
<--- Score

118. How was the detailed process map generated, verified, and validated?
<--- Score

119. How do you measure the operational performance of your key work systems and processes, including productivity, cycle time, and other appropriate measures of process effectiveness, efficiency, and innovation?
<--- Score

120. What were the crucial 'moments of truth' on the process map?
<--- Score

121. How do you implement and manage your work processes to ensure that they meet design requirements?
<--- Score

122. Where is desktop application data gathered?
<--- Score

123. Are you missing desktop application opportunities?
<--- Score

124. Is the required desktop application data gathered?
<--- Score

125. What data is gathered?
<--- Score

126. What are evaluation criteria for the output?
<--- Score

127. Identify an operational issue in your organization, for example, could a particular task be done more quickly or more efficiently by desktop application?
<--- Score

128. Where is the data coming from to measure compliance?
<--- Score

129. How will the data be checked for quality?
<--- Score

130. How is the data gathered?
<--- Score

131. What is the cost of poor quality as supported by the team's analysis?
<--- Score

132. How much data can be collected in the given timeframe?

<--- Score

133. Who is involved in the management review process?
<--- Score

134. What are the desktop application design outputs?
<--- Score

135. What output to create?
<--- Score

136. Is the suppliers process defined and controlled?
<--- Score

Add up total points for this section:
_____ = Total points for this section

Divided by: _____ (number of statements answered) = _____
Average score for this section

Transfer your score to the desktop application Index at the beginning of the Self-Assessment.

CRITERION #5: IMPROVE:

INTENT: Develop a practical solution.
Innovate, establish and test the
solution and to measure the results.

In my belief, the answer to this
question is clearly defined:

5 Strongly Agree

4 Agree

3 Neutral

2 Disagree

1 Strongly Disagree

1. What lessons, if any, from a pilot were incorporated
into the design of the full-scale solution?
<--- Score

2. Have you identified breakpoints and/or risk
tolerances that will trigger broad consideration of
a potential need for intervention or modification of
strategy?
<--- Score

3. How do you improve desktop application service perception, and satisfaction?
<--- Score

4. How can skill-level changes improve desktop application?
<--- Score

5. Can you integrate quality management and risk management?
<--- Score

6. Who manages desktop application risk?
<--- Score

7. At what point will vulnerability assessments be performed once desktop application is put into production (e.g., ongoing Risk Management after implementation)?
<--- Score

8. How do you go about comparing desktop application approaches/solutions?
<--- Score

9. Explorations of the frontiers of desktop application will help you build influence, improve desktop application, optimize decision making, and sustain change, what is your approach?
<--- Score

10. What are the implications of the one critical desktop application decision 10 minutes, 10 months, and 10 years from now?
<--- Score

11. How do you measure risk?
<--- Score

12. Who will be responsible for making the decisions to include or exclude requested changes once desktop application is underway?
<--- Score

13. What area needs the greatest improvement?
<--- Score

14. What desktop application improvements can be made?
<--- Score

15. Would you develop a desktop application Communication Strategy?
<--- Score

16. Is any desktop application documentation required?
<--- Score

17. Does a good decision guarantee a good outcome?
<--- Score

18. Are risk triggers captured?
<--- Score

19. What is the risk?
<--- Score

20. What tools were most useful during the improve phase?
<--- Score

21. Who will be responsible for documenting the desktop application requirements in detail?
<--- Score

22. How are policy decisions made and where?
<--- Score

23. How do you keep improving desktop application?
<--- Score

24. In the past few months, what is the smallest change you have made that has had the biggest positive result? What was it about that small change that produced the large return?
<--- Score

25. Are procedures documented for managing desktop application risks?
<--- Score

26. Are risk management tasks balanced centrally and locally?
<--- Score

27. How are desktop application risks managed?
<--- Score

28. Can the solution be designed and implemented within an acceptable time period?
<--- Score

29. Is the desktop application solution sustainable?
<--- Score

30. Is the desktop application risk managed?

<--- Score

31. What to do with the results or outcomes of measurements?
<--- Score

32. Where do you need desktop application improvement?
<--- Score

33. Where do the desktop application decisions reside?
<--- Score

34. Do you need to do a usability evaluation?
<--- Score

35. How will you know that you have improved?
<--- Score

36. What are the expected desktop application results?
<--- Score

37. How will you recognize and celebrate results?
<--- Score

38. Who are the key stakeholders for the desktop application evaluation?
<--- Score

39. What do you want to improve?
<--- Score

40. Is there a high likelihood that any recommendations will achieve their intended results?

<--- Score

41. Who manages supplier risk management in your organization?
<--- Score

42. How will you measure the results?
<--- Score

43. What assumptions are made about the solution and approach?
<--- Score

44. Who controls key decisions that will be made?
<--- Score

45. What should a proof of concept or pilot accomplish?
<--- Score

46. Are the key business and technology risks being managed?
<--- Score

47. Who makes the desktop application decisions in your organization?
<--- Score

48. What can you do to improve?
<--- Score

49. How scalable is your desktop application solution?
<--- Score

50. How do you improve productivity?
<--- Score

51. What is desktop application risk?
<--- Score

52. What are the desktop application security risks?
<--- Score

53. How is continuous improvement applied to risk management?
<--- Score

54. What needs improvement? Why?
<--- Score

55. When you map the key players in your own work and the types/domains of relationships with them, which relationships do you find easy and which challenging, and why?
<--- Score

56. What strategies for desktop application improvement are successful?
<--- Score

57. Is the solution technically practical?
<--- Score

58. Is the desktop application documentation thorough?
<--- Score

59. Do you have the optimal project management team structure?
<--- Score

60. Is there any other desktop application solution?

<--- Score

61. How does your organization evaluate strategic desktop application success?
<--- Score

62. How do you deal with desktop application risk?
<--- Score

63. What is the magnitude of the improvements?
<--- Score

64. What tools were used to evaluate the potential solutions?
<--- Score

65. What are the affordable desktop application risks?
<--- Score

66. How do you manage desktop application risk?
<--- Score

67. How is knowledge sharing about risk management improved?
<--- Score

68. What tools do you use once you have decided on a desktop application strategy and more importantly how do you choose?
<--- Score

69. How do you decide how much to remunerate an employee?
<--- Score

70. How can the phases of desktop application

development be identified?
<--- Score

71. Who do you report desktop application results to?
<--- Score

72. What practices helps your organization to develop its capacity to recognize patterns?
<--- Score

73. Will the controls trigger any other risks?
<--- Score

74. desktop application risk decisions: whose call Is It?
<--- Score

75. What resources are required for the improvement efforts?
<--- Score

76. Risk events: what are the things that could go wrong?
<--- Score

77. How risky is your organization?
<--- Score

78. What are your current levels and trends in key measures or indicators of workforce and leader development?
<--- Score

79. Is supporting desktop application documentation required?
<--- Score

80. Do you cover the five essential competencies: Communication, Collaboration,Innovation, Adaptability, and Leadership that improve an organizations ability to leverage the new desktop application in a volatile global economy?
<--- Score

81. Do those selected for the desktop application team have a good general understanding of what desktop application is all about?
<--- Score

82. Are the risks fully understood, reasonable and manageable?
<--- Score

83. Is the scope clearly documented?
<--- Score

84. Do vendor agreements bring new compliance risk ?
<--- Score

85. Are you assessing desktop application and risk?
<--- Score

86. Which of the recognised risks out of all risks can be most likely transferred?
<--- Score

87. Who will be using the results of the measurement activities?
<--- Score

88. What current systems have to be understood and/ or changed?

<--- Score

89. How do you improve your likelihood of success ?
<--- Score

90. How will you know that a change is an improvement?
<--- Score

91. To what extent does management recognize desktop application as a tool to increase the results?
<--- Score

92. What were the criteria for evaluating a desktop application pilot?
<--- Score

93. How do the desktop application results compare with the performance of your competitors and other organizations with similar offerings?
<--- Score

94. Is desktop application documentation maintained?
<--- Score

95. How do you measure progress and evaluate training effectiveness?
<--- Score

96. What actually has to improve and by how much?
<--- Score

97. Risk factors: what are the characteristics of desktop application that make it risky?
<--- Score

98. How significant is the improvement in the eyes of the end user?
<--- Score

99. Is risk periodically assessed?
<--- Score

100. What tools were used to tap into the creativity and encourage 'outside the box' thinking?
<--- Score

101. Have you achieved desktop application improvements?
<--- Score

102. What criteria will you use to assess your desktop application risks?
<--- Score

103. Are the most efficient solutions problem-specific?
<--- Score

104. What were the underlying assumptions on the cost-benefit analysis?
<--- Score

105. Are events managed to resolution?
<--- Score

106. Who are the desktop application decision-makers?
<--- Score

107. Do you combine technical expertise with business knowledge and desktop application Key

topics include lifecycles, development approaches, requirements and how to make a business case?
<--- Score

108. Who are the desktop application decision makers?
<--- Score

109. Is the measure of success for desktop application understandable to a variety of people?
<--- Score

110. Who controls the risk?
<--- Score

111. Why improve in the first place?
<--- Score

112. How do you mitigate desktop application risk?
<--- Score

113. How can you better manage risk?
<--- Score

114. How do you define the solutions' scope?
<--- Score

115. How will you know when its improved?
<--- Score

116. What went well, what should change, what can improve?
<--- Score

117. What alternative responses are available to manage risk?

<--- Score

118. Are decisions made in a timely manner?
<--- Score

119. What is needed to design and pilot an enterprise App store for distributing mobile and desktop applications?
<--- Score

120. How can you improve performance?
<--- Score

121. How do you link measurement and risk?
<--- Score

122. What are the concrete desktop application results?
<--- Score

123. How do you manage and improve your desktop application work systems to deliver customer value and achieve organizational success and sustainability?
<--- Score

124. How do you measure improved desktop application service perception, and satisfaction?
<--- Score

125. What improvements have been achieved?
<--- Score

126. For decision problems, how do you develop a decision statement?
<--- Score

127. Can you identify any significant risks or exposures to desktop application third- parties (vendors, service providers, alliance partners etc) that concern you?
<--- Score

128. Which desktop application solution is appropriate?
<--- Score

129. Was a desktop application charter developed?
<--- Score

130. How can you improve desktop application?
<--- Score

Add up total points for this section:
_____ = Total points for this section

Divided by: _____ (number of statements answered) = _____
Average score for this section

Transfer your score to the desktop application Index at the beginning of the Self-Assessment.

CRITERION #6: CONTROL:

In my belief, the answer to this question is clearly defined:

5 Strongly Agree

4 Agree

3 Neutral

2 Disagree

1 Strongly Disagree

1. What is the standard for acceptable desktop application performance?
<--- Score

2. How will new or emerging customer needs/ requirements be checked/communicated to orient the process toward meeting the new specifications and continually reducing variation?
<--- Score

3. Are new process steps, standards, and documentation ingrained into normal operations?
<--- Score

4. What are your results for key measures or indicators of the accomplishment of your desktop application strategy and action plans, including building and strengthening core competencies?
<--- Score

5. How do you establish and deploy modified action plans if circumstances require a shift in plans and rapid execution of new plans?
<--- Score

6. What are the key elements of your desktop application performance improvement system, including your evaluation, organizational learning, and innovation processes?
<--- Score

7. How will the process owner and team be able to hold the gains?
<--- Score

8. Can support from partners be adjusted?
<--- Score

9. What do your reports reflect?
<--- Score

10. What desktop application standards are applicable?
<--- Score

11. How will the day-to-day responsibilities for monitoring and continual improvement be transferred from the improvement team to the process owner?
<--- Score

12. How do you plan for the cost of succession?
<--- Score

13. How will desktop application decisions be made and monitored?
<--- Score

14. How do controls support value?
<--- Score

15. Are pertinent alerts monitored, analyzed and distributed to appropriate personnel?
<--- Score

16. Do the desktop application decisions you make today help people and the planet tomorrow?
<--- Score

17. In the case of a desktop application project, the criteria for the audit derive from implementation objectives, an audit of a desktop application project involves assessing whether the recommendations outlined for implementation have been met, can you track that any desktop application project is implemented as planned, and is it working?
<--- Score

18. Will any special training be provided for results interpretation?
<--- Score

19. Does the desktop application performance meet the customer's requirements?
<--- Score

20. How do you select, collect, align, and integrate desktop application data and information for tracking daily operations and overall organizational performance, including progress relative to strategic objectives and action plans?
<--- Score

21. What is the control/monitoring plan?
<--- Score

22. What are you attempting to measure/monitor?
<--- Score

23. How might the group capture best practices and lessons learned so as to leverage improvements?
<--- Score

24. Is knowledge gained on process shared and institutionalized?
<--- Score

25. How widespread is its use?
<--- Score

26. What are customers monitoring?
<--- Score

27. Are the planned controls working?
<--- Score

28. What are the critical parameters to watch?

<--- Score

29. What other systems, operations, processes, and infrastructures (hiring practices, staffing, training, incentives/rewards, metrics/dashboards/scorecards, etc.) need updates, additions, changes, or deletions in order to facilitate knowledge transfer and improvements?
<--- Score

30. Are you measuring, monitoring and predicting desktop application activities to optimize operations and profitability, and enhancing outcomes?
<--- Score

31. Implementation Planning: is a pilot needed to test the changes before a full roll out occurs?
<--- Score

32. Is there a documented and implemented monitoring plan?
<--- Score

33. What is your theory of human motivation, and how does your compensation plan fit with that view?
<--- Score

34. Are controls in place and consistently applied?
<--- Score

35. Will existing staff require re-training, for example, to learn new business processes?
<--- Score

36. How is desktop application project cost planned, managed, monitored?

<--- Score

37. Who controls critical resources?
<--- Score

38. Is there a control plan in place for sustaining improvements (short and long-term)?
<--- Score

39. Has the desktop application value of standards been quantified?
<--- Score

40. Who is the desktop application process owner?
<--- Score

41. Do you monitor the effectiveness of your desktop application activities?
<--- Score

42. Are documented procedures clear and easy to follow for the operators?
<--- Score

43. Who has control over resources?
<--- Score

44. What should the next improvement project be that is related to desktop application?
<--- Score

45. Act/Adjust: What Do you Need to Do Differently?
<--- Score

46. How will the process owner verify improvement in present and future sigma levels, process capabilities?

<--- Score

47. How will report readings be checked to effectively monitor performance?
<--- Score

48. Is reporting being used or needed?
<--- Score

49. Are suggested corrective/restorative actions indicated on the response plan for known causes to problems that might surface?
<--- Score

50. Have new or revised work instructions resulted?
<--- Score

51. Does the response plan contain a definite closed loop continual improvement scheme (e.g., plan-do-check-act)?
<--- Score

52. How will input, process, and output variables be checked to detect for sub-optimal conditions?
<--- Score

53. Is a response plan established and deployed?
<--- Score

54. Who sets the desktop application standards?
<--- Score

55. Will your goals reflect your program budget?
<--- Score

56. What other areas of the group might benefit

from the desktop application team's improvements, knowledge, and learning?

<--- Score

57. Is there documentation that will support the successful operation of the improvement?

<--- Score

58. Does a troubleshooting guide exist or is it needed?

<--- Score

59. How likely is the current desktop application plan to come in on schedule or on budget?

<--- Score

60. What is the best design framework for desktop application organization now that, in a post industrial-age if the top-down, command and control model is no longer relevant?

<--- Score

61. Is there a standardized process?

<--- Score

62. Is a response plan in place for when the input, process, or output measures indicate an 'out-of-control' condition?

<--- Score

63. How will you measure your QA plan's effectiveness?

<--- Score

64. Is new knowledge gained imbedded in the response plan?

<--- Score

65. Do you monitor the desktop application decisions made and fine tune them as they evolve?
<--- Score

66. Are the planned controls in place?
<--- Score

67. What do you measure to verify effectiveness gains?
<--- Score

68. Has the improved process and its steps been standardized?
<--- Score

69. How do you spread information?
<--- Score

70. What quality tools were useful in the control phase?
<--- Score

71. Is there an action plan in case of emergencies?
<--- Score

72. Are the desktop application standards challenging?
<--- Score

73. How is change control managed?
<--- Score

74. You may have created your quality measures at a time when you lacked resources, technology wasn't up to the required standard, or low service levels

were the industry norm. Have those circumstances changed?
<--- Score

75. Does job training on the documented procedures need to be part of the process team's education and training?
<--- Score

76. What are the performance and scale of the desktop application tools?
<--- Score

77. Are operating procedures consistent?
<--- Score

78. Who will be in control?
<--- Score

79. What do you stand for--and what are you against?
<--- Score

80. How do your controls stack up?
<--- Score

81. Where do ideas that reach policy makers and planners as proposals for desktop application strengthening and reform actually originate?
<--- Score

82. Is there a recommended audit plan for routine surveillance inspections of desktop application's gains?
<--- Score

83. What are the known security controls?

<--- Score

84. How do you plan on providing proper recognition and disclosure of supporting companies?
<--- Score

85. Does desktop application appropriately measure and monitor risk?
<--- Score

86. Against what alternative is success being measured?
<--- Score

87. How do senior leaders actions reflect a commitment to the organizations desktop application values?
<--- Score

88. Can you adapt and adjust to changing desktop application situations?
<--- Score

89. What should you measure to verify efficiency gains?
<--- Score

90. What is your plan to assess your security risks?
<--- Score

91. Is there a desktop application Communication plan covering who needs to get what information when?
<--- Score

92. Is there a transfer of ownership and knowledge

to process owner and process team tasked with the responsibilities.
<--- Score

93. What is the recommended frequency of auditing?
<--- Score

94. Are there documented procedures?
<--- Score

95. How can you best use all of your knowledge repositories to enhance learning and sharing?
<--- Score

96. How do you encourage people to take control and responsibility?
<--- Score

97. Do the viable solutions scale to future needs?
<--- Score

98. Will the team be available to assist members in planning investigations?
<--- Score

99. What key inputs and outputs are being measured on an ongoing basis?
<--- Score

100. Is the desktop application test/monitoring cost justified?
<--- Score

Add up total points for this section:
_ _ _ _ _ = Total points for this section

Divided by: _____ (number of
statements answered) = _____
Average score for this section

Transfer your score to the desktop
application Index at the beginning of
the Self-Assessment.

CRITERION #7: SUSTAIN:

INTENT: Retain the benefits.

In my belief, the answer to this
question is clearly defined:

5 Strongly Agree

4 Agree

3 Neutral

2 Disagree

1 Strongly Disagree

1. What business benefits will desktop application
goals deliver if achieved?
<--- Score

2. If there were zero limitations, what would you do
differently?
<--- Score

3. Do you have the right capabilities and capacities?
<--- Score

4. What did you miss in the interview for the worst hire you ever made?
<--- Score

5. In the past year, what have you done (or could you have done) to increase the accurate perception of your company/brand as ethical and honest?
<--- Score

6. What desktop application skills are most important?
<--- Score

7. How will you motivate the stakeholders with the least vested interest?
<--- Score

8. In retrospect, of the projects that you pulled the plug on, what percent do you wish had been allowed to keep going, and what percent do you wish had ended earlier?
<--- Score

9. How do you know if you are successful?
<--- Score

10. Do you have an implicit bias for capital investments over people investments?
<--- Score

11. What could happen if you do not do it?
<--- Score

12. What should you stop doing?
<--- Score

13. Is there any reason to believe the opposite of my

current belief?
<--- Score

14. If you had to leave your organization for a year and the only communication you could have with employees/colleagues was a single paragraph, what would you write?
<--- Score

15. What new services of functionality will be implemented next with desktop application ?
<--- Score

16. Have new benefits been realized?
<--- Score

17. Do you think desktop application accomplishes the goals you expect it to accomplish?
<--- Score

18. What is your competitive advantage?
<--- Score

19. What is the big desktop application idea?
<--- Score

20. Do you see more potential in people than they do in themselves?
<--- Score

21. How do you foster innovation?
<--- Score

22. What are your most important goals for the strategic desktop application objectives?
<--- Score

23. How do you manage desktop application Knowledge Management (KM)?
<--- Score

24. Why will customers want to buy your organizations products/services?
<--- Score

25. Whose voice (department, ethnic group, women, older workers, etc) might you have missed hearing from in your company, and how might you amplify this voice to create positive momentum for your business?
<--- Score

26. How do you cross-sell and up-sell your desktop application success?
<--- Score

27. Have benefits been optimized with all key stakeholders?
<--- Score

28. Do you have the right people on the bus?
<--- Score

29. Do desktop application rules make a reasonable demand on a users capabilities?
<--- Score

30. How can you negotiate desktop application successfully with a stubborn boss, an irate client, or a deceitful coworker?
<--- Score

31. Instead of going to current contacts for new ideas, what if you reconnected with dormant contacts-- the people you used to know? If you were going reactivate a dormant tie, who would it be?
<--- Score

32. What are the long-term desktop application goals?
<--- Score

33. Which individuals, teams or departments will be involved in desktop application?
<--- Score

34. Are you using a design thinking approach and integrating Innovation, desktop application Experience, and Brand Value?
<--- Score

35. What is the purpose of desktop application in relation to the mission?
<--- Score

36. Do you know what you are doing? And who do you call if you don't?
<--- Score

37. What trophy do you want on your mantle?
<--- Score

38. What trouble can you get into?
<--- Score

39. What goals did you miss?
<--- Score

40. Is there any existing desktop application

governance structure?
<--- Score

41. Which functions and people interact with the supplier and or customer?
<--- Score

42. Why should people listen to you?
<--- Score

43. How do you track customer value, profitability or financial return, organizational success, and sustainability?
<--- Score

44. What knowledge, skills and characteristics mark a good desktop application project manager?
<--- Score

45. What is the kind of project structure that would be appropriate for your desktop application project, should it be formal and complex, or can it be less formal and relatively simple?
<--- Score

46. How will you know that the desktop application project has been successful?
<--- Score

47. What is something you believe that nearly no one agrees with you on?
<--- Score

48. What will be the consequences to the stakeholder (financial, reputation etc) if desktop application does not go ahead or fails to deliver the objectives?

<--- Score

49. Think of your desktop application project, what are the main functions?
<--- Score

50. How will you ensure you get what you expected?
<--- Score

51. How do you listen to customers to obtain actionable information?
<--- Score

52. If you do not follow, then how to lead?
<--- Score

53. What are the short and long-term desktop application goals?
<--- Score

54. What happens at your organization when people fail?
<--- Score

55. How can you become the company that would put you out of business?
<--- Score

56. Why is it important to have senior management support for a desktop application project?
<--- Score

57. What relationships among desktop application trends do you perceive?
<--- Score

58. How do you stay inspired?
<--- Score

59. How long will it take to change?
<--- Score

60. What have you done to protect your business from competitive encroachment?
<--- Score

61. What is an unauthorized commitment?
<--- Score

62. Which models, tools and techniques are necessary?
<--- Score

63. What are you trying to prove to yourself, and how might it be hijacking your life and business success?
<--- Score

64. Why should you adopt a desktop application framework?
<--- Score

65. Are assumptions made in desktop application stated explicitly?
<--- Score

66. What have been your experiences in defining long range desktop application goals?
<--- Score

67. What are internal and external desktop application relations?
<--- Score

68. Who is on the team?
<--- Score

69. What desktop application modifications can you make work for you?
<--- Score

70. Who will be responsible for deciding whether desktop application goes ahead or not after the initial investigations?
<--- Score

71. What are the rules and assumptions your industry operates under? What if the opposite were true?
<--- Score

72. What are the key enablers to make this desktop application move?
<--- Score

73. What are your personal philosophies regarding desktop application and how do they influence your work?
<--- Score

74. How will you insure seamless interoperability of desktop application moving forward?
<--- Score

75. Did your employees make progress today?
<--- Score

76. Can you break it down?
<--- Score

77. What are the potential basics of desktop application fraud?
<--- Score

78. What is your BATNA (best alternative to a negotiated agreement)?
<--- Score

79. If you had to rebuild your organization without any traditional competitive advantages (i.e., no killer technology, promising research, innovative product/ service delivery model, etcetera), how would your people have to approach their work and collaborate together in order to create the necessary conditions for success?
<--- Score

80. How much does desktop application help?
<--- Score

81. What is your formula for success in desktop application ?
<--- Score

82. How do you accomplish your long range desktop application goals?
<--- Score

83. Is there a work around that you can use?
<--- Score

84. What threat is desktop application addressing?
<--- Score

85. Is a desktop application breakthrough on the horizon?

<--- Score

86. Are you maintaining a past–present–future perspective throughout the desktop application discussion?
<--- Score

87. What was the last experiment you ran?
<--- Score

88. What information is critical to your organization that your executives are ignoring?
<--- Score

89. Can you maintain your growth without detracting from the factors that have contributed to your success?
<--- Score

90. Are new benefits received and understood?
<--- Score

91. Operational - will it work?
<--- Score

92. Who are your customers?
<--- Score

93. What are the top 3 things at the forefront of your desktop application agendas for the next 3 years?
<--- Score

94. How likely is it that a customer would recommend your company to a friend or colleague?
<--- Score

95. How do you determine the key elements that affect desktop application workforce satisfaction, how are these elements determined for different workforce groups and segments?
<--- Score

96. Who, on the executive team or the board, has spoken to a customer recently?
<--- Score

97. Are your responses positive or negative?
<--- Score

98. Do you feel that more should be done in the desktop application area?
<--- Score

99. Is your basic point _____ or _____?
<--- Score

100. How do you keep records, of what?
<--- Score

101. Where can you break convention?
<--- Score

102. What are the essentials of internal desktop application management?
<--- Score

103. Are the assumptions believable and achievable?
<--- Score

104. Who is responsible for ensuring appropriate resources (time, people and money) are allocated to desktop application?

<--- Score

105. What happens when a new employee joins the organization?
<--- Score

106. How do you proactively clarify deliverables and desktop application quality expectations?
<--- Score

107. Who have you, as a company, historically been when you've been at your best?
<--- Score

108. How do you provide a safe environment -physically and emotionally?
<--- Score

109. Is the desktop application organization completing tasks effectively and efficiently?
<--- Score

110. What is the overall business strategy?
<--- Score

111. How do you lead with desktop application in mind?
<--- Score

112. What does your signature ensure?
<--- Score

113. What is a feasible sequencing of reform initiatives over time?
<--- Score

114. How do you foster the skills, knowledge, talents, attributes, and characteristics you want to have?
<--- Score

115. How much contingency will be available in the budget?
<--- Score

116. How do you maintain desktop application's Integrity?
<--- Score

117. At what moment would you think; Will I get fired?
<--- Score

118. Ask yourself: how would you do this work if you only had one staff member to do it?
<--- Score

119. Are you / should you be revolutionary or evolutionary?
<--- Score

120. Are you relevant? Will you be relevant five years from now? Ten?
<--- Score

121. How do you keep the momentum going?
<--- Score

122. What potential megatrends could make your business model obsolete?
<--- Score

123. How do you make it meaningful in connecting desktop application with what users do day-to-day?

<--- Score

124. If no one would ever find out about your accomplishments, how would you lead differently?
<--- Score

125. Who do you think the world wants your organization to be?
<--- Score

126. What are the challenges?
<--- Score

127. Why not do desktop application?
<--- Score

128. Are you satisfied with your current role? If not, what is missing from it?
<--- Score

129. How do you deal with desktop application changes?
<--- Score

130. Who else should you help?
<--- Score

131. How do you engage the workforce, in addition to satisfying them?
<--- Score

132. Is desktop application dependent on the successful delivery of a current project?
<--- Score

133. How are you doing compared to your industry?

<--- Score

134. Do you say no to customers for no reason?
<--- Score

135. Who will provide the final approval of desktop application deliverables?
<--- Score

136. Can the schedule be done in the given time?
<--- Score

137. In a project to restructure desktop application outcomes, which stakeholders would you involve?
<--- Score

138. Marketing budgets are tighter, consumers are more skeptical, and social media has changed forever the way we talk about desktop application, how do you gain traction?
<--- Score

139. How do senior leaders deploy your organizations vision and values through your leadership system, to the workforce, to key suppliers and partners, and to customers and other stakeholders, as appropriate?
<--- Score

140. How is implementation research currently incorporated into each of your goals?
<--- Score

141. What unique value proposition (UVP) do you offer?
<--- Score

142. Are all key stakeholders present at all Structured Walkthroughs?
<--- Score

143. What is the craziest thing you can do?
<--- Score

144. Who do we want your customers to become?
<--- Score

145. Who do you want your customers to become?
<--- Score

146. What are the usability implications of desktop application actions?
<--- Score

147. Who are the key stakeholders?
<--- Score

148. Do you have enough freaky customers in your portfolio pushing you to the limit day in and day out?
<--- Score

149. What is the recommended frequency of auditing?
<--- Score

150. Is your strategy driving your strategy? Or is the way in which you allocate resources driving your strategy?
<--- Score

151. What are the gaps in your knowledge and experience?
<--- Score

152. Would you rather sell to knowledgeable and informed customers or to uninformed customers?
<--- Score

153. Are you paying enough attention to the partners your company depends on to succeed?
<--- Score

154. What counts that you are not counting?
<--- Score

155. Are you making progress, and are you making progress as desktop application leaders?
<--- Score

156. Can you do all this work?
<--- Score

157. Who uses your product in ways you never expected?
<--- Score

158. What is the range of capabilities?
<--- Score

159. Who is responsible for errors?
<--- Score

160. What must you excel at?
<--- Score

161. What would have to be true for the option on the table to be the best possible choice?
<--- Score

162. Has implementation been effective in reaching

specified objectives so far?
<--- Score

163. What do we do when new problems arise?
<--- Score

164. What would you recommend your friend do if he/she were facing this dilemma?
<--- Score

165. Are there any activities that you can take off your to do list?
<--- Score

166. How do you set desktop application stretch targets and how do you get people to not only participate in setting these stretch targets but also that they strive to achieve these?
<--- Score

167. What is the overall talent health of your organization as a whole at senior levels, and for each organization reporting to a member of the Senior Leadership Team?
<--- Score

168. How do you go about securing desktop application?
<--- Score

169. Is maximizing desktop application protection the same as minimizing desktop application loss?
<--- Score

170. How do you create buy-in?
<--- Score

171. Will there be any necessary staff changes (redundancies or new hires)?
<--- Score

172. If you find that you havent accomplished one of the goals for one of the steps of the desktop application strategy, what will you do to fix it?
<--- Score

173. What is your question? Why?
<--- Score

174. Is a desktop application team work effort in place?
<--- Score

175. How do customers see your organization?
<--- Score

176. Is the impact that desktop application has shown?
<--- Score

177. How can you become more high-tech but still be high touch?
<--- Score

178. What management system can you use to leverage the desktop application experience, ideas, and concerns of the people closest to the work to be done?
<--- Score

179. What one word do you want to own in the minds of your customers, employees, and partners?

<--- Score

180. What are the primary differences between desktop applications and Windows Universal apps?
<--- Score

181. Whom among your colleagues do you trust, and for what?
<--- Score

182. What are strategies for increasing support and reducing opposition?
<--- Score

183. How important is desktop application to the user organizations mission?
<--- Score

184. Why do and why don't your customers like your organization?
<--- Score

185. What is it like to work for you?
<--- Score

186. How do you use desktop applications from AWS Marketplace?
<--- Score

187. What is the funding source for this project?
<--- Score

188. What is the estimated value of the project?
<--- Score

189. What happens if you do not have enough funding?

<--- Score

190. Do you have past desktop application successes?

<--- Score

191. Who will determine interim and final deadlines?

<--- Score

192. Which desktop application goals are the most important?

<--- Score

193. What projects are going on in the organization today, and what resources are those projects using from the resource pools?

<--- Score

194. How can you incorporate support to ensure safe and effective use of desktop application into the services that you provide?

<--- Score

195. What are current desktop application paradigms?

<--- Score

196. Are the criteria for selecting recommendations stated?

<--- Score

197. If you weren't already in this business, would you enter it today? And if not, what are you going to do about it?

<--- Score

198. If you were responsible for initiating and implementing major changes in your organization, what steps might you take to ensure acceptance of those changes?
<--- Score

199. If your company went out of business tomorrow, would anyone who doesn't get a paycheck here care?
<--- Score

200. How does desktop application integrate with other stakeholder initiatives?
<--- Score

201. How do you assess the desktop application pitfalls that are inherent in implementing it?
<--- Score

202. What are the business goals desktop application is aiming to achieve?
<--- Score

203. What is effective desktop application?
<--- Score

204. If your customer were your grandmother, would you tell her to buy what you're selling?
<--- Score

205. Do you know who is a friend or a foe?
<--- Score

206. Is it economical; do you have the time and money?
<--- Score

207. Who will manage the integration of tools?
<--- Score

208. Were lessons learned captured and communicated?
<--- Score

209. Who are four people whose careers you have enhanced?
<--- Score

210. Political -is anyone trying to undermine this project?
<--- Score

211. Who is the main stakeholder, with ultimate responsibility for driving desktop application forward?
<--- Score

212. Are you changing as fast as the world around you?
<--- Score

213. If you got fired and a new hire took your place, what would she do different?
<--- Score

Add up total points for this section:
_____ = Total points for this section

Divided by: _____ (number of statements answered) = _____
Average score for this section

Transfer your score to the desktop application Index at the beginning of

the Self-Assessment.

Desktop Application and Managing Projects, Criteria for Project Managers:

1.0 Initiating Process Group: Desktop Application

1. How is each deliverable reviewed, verified, and validated?

2. Were decisions made in a timely manner?

3. How well did you do?

4. Who is performing the work of the Desktop Application project?

5. What were things that you did very well and want to do the same again on the next Desktop Application project?

6. In which Desktop Application project management process group is the detailed Desktop Application project budget created?

7. Which of six sigmas dmaic phases focuses on the measurement of internal process that affect factors that are critical to quality?

8. How will you do it?

9. First of all, should any action be taken?

10. What will be the pressing issues of tomorrow?

11. Were resources available as planned?

12. How can you make your needs known?

13. Information sharing?

14. What is the stake of others in your Desktop Application project?

15. Does the Desktop Application project team have enough people to execute the Desktop Application project plan?

16. What input will you be required to provide the Desktop Application project team?

17. What is the NEXT thing to do?

18. Professionals want to know what is expected from them what are the deliverables?

19. What are the overarching issues of your organization?

20. Measurable - are the targets measurable?

1.1 Project Charter: Desktop Application

21. How are Desktop Application projects different from operations?

22. Are you building in-house ?

23. Where does all this information come from?

24. Fit with other Products Compliments – Cannibalizes?

25. What ideas do you have for initial tests of change (PDSA cycles)?

26. Desktop Application project background: what is the primary motivation for this Desktop Application project?

27. Who is the Desktop Application project Manager?

28. Is it an improvement over existing products?

29. Market – identify products market, including whether it is outside of the objective: what is the purpose of the program or Desktop Application project?

30. What are you striving to accomplish (measurable goal(s))?

31. What are you trying to accomplish?

32. Assumptions and constraints: what assumptions were made in defining the Desktop Application project?

33. What is the most common tool for helping define the detail?

34. Dependent Desktop Application projects: what Desktop Application projects must be underway or completed before this Desktop Application project can be successful?

35. Desktop Application project deliverables: what is the Desktop Application project going to produce?

36. Is time of the essence?

37. Who will take notes, document decisions?

38. How high should you set your goals?

39. Why do you manage integration?

40. Avoid costs, improve service, and/ or comply with a mandate?

1.2 Stakeholder Register: Desktop Application

41. Who wants to talk about Security?

42. Who are the stakeholders?

43. Who is managing stakeholder engagement?

44. How big is the gap?

45. What & Why?

46. What opportunities exist to provide communications?

47. How should employers make voices heard?

48. What are the major Desktop Application project milestones requiring communications or providing communications opportunities?

49. Is your organization ready for change?

50. How will reports be created?

51. How much influence do they have on the Desktop Application project?

52. What is the power of the stakeholder?

1.3 Stakeholder Analysis Matrix: Desktop Application

53. Marketing - reach, distribution, awareness?

54. Processes, systems, it, communications?

55. Who will obstruct/hinder the Desktop Application project if they are not involved?

56. What do you need to appraise?

57. Who is directly responsible for decisions on issues important to the Desktop Application project?

58. Who is most dependent on the resources at stake?

59. Is there a clear description of the scope of practice of the Desktop Application projects educators?

60. Accreditations, qualifications, certifications?

61. How much do resources cost?

62. Price, value, quality?

63. Why do you care?

64. Information and research?

65. Is there evidence that demonstrates the impact of education on the Desktop Application projects outcomes?

66. How do you manage Desktop Application project Risk?

67. Geographical, export, import?

68. Who influences whom?

69. Supporters; who are the supporters?

70. Who are potential allies and opponents?

71. What is the range you need to look at?

2.0 Planning Process Group: Desktop Application

72. To what extent have the target population and participants made the activities own, taking an active role in it?

73. In what way has the Desktop Application project come up with innovative measures for problem-solving?

74. What good practices or successful experiences or transferable examples have been identified?

75. What do you need to do?

76. Will you be replaced?

77. Is the schedule for the set products being met?

78. What will you do?

79. If a task is partitionable, is this a sufficient condition to reduce the Desktop Application project duration?

80. How should needs be met?

81. If task x starts two days late, what is the effect on the Desktop Application project end date?

82. To what extent do the intervention objectives and strategies of the Desktop Application project respond

to your organizations plans?

83. What is a Software Development Life Cycle (SDLC)?

84. Just how important is your work to the overall success of the Desktop Application project?

85. Did you read it correctly?

86. Why do it Desktop Application projects fail?

87. How are the principles of aid effectiveness (ownership, alignment, management for development results and mutual responsibility) being applied in the Desktop Application project?

88. How well will the chosen processes produce the expected results?

89. What is the difference between the early schedule and late schedule?

90. To what extent is the program helping to influence your organizations policy framework?

2.1 Project Management Plan: Desktop Application

91. What went right?

92. How do you manage integration?

93. What worked well?

94. Who is the Desktop Application project Manager?

95. How do you manage time?

96. What are the assigned resources?

97. What went wrong?

98. Development trends and opportunities. What if the positive direction and vision of your organization causes expected trends to change?

99. When is a Desktop Application project management plan created?

100. Who is the sponsor?

101. Are comparable cost estimates used for comparing, screening and selecting alternative plans, and has a reasonable cost estimate been developed for the recommended plan?

102. What would you do differently what did not work?

103. What happened during the process that you found interesting?

104. How do you organize the costs in the Desktop Application project management plan?

105. What is risk management?

106. Does the selected plan protect privacy?

107. Are the proposed Desktop Application project purposes different than a previously authorized Desktop Application project?

108. What are the deliverables?

109. Do the proposed changes from the Desktop Application project include any significant risks to safety?

2.2 Scope Management Plan: Desktop Application

110. Are there procedures in place to effectively manage interdependencies with other Desktop Application projects, systems, Vendors and your organizations work effort?

111. Are schedule deliverables actually delivered?

112. What are the risks that could significantly affect the scope of the Desktop Application project?

113. Are the payment terms being followed?

114. How will scope changes be identified and classified?

115. How difficult will it be to do specific activities on this Desktop Application project?

116. Can each item be appropriately scheduled?

117. For which criterion is it tolerable not to meet the original parameters?

118. Have adequate procedures been put in place for Desktop Application project communication and status reporting across Desktop Application project boundaries (for example interdependent software development among interfacing systems)?

119. Are the budget estimates reasonable?

120. Do you keep stake holders informed?

121. Have all involved Desktop Application project stakeholders and work groups committed to the Desktop Application project?

122. Are the quality tools and methods identified in the Quality Plan appropriate to the Desktop Application project?

123. Does the title convey to the reader the essence of the Desktop Application project?

124. Are the Desktop Application project team members located locally to the users/stakeholders?

125. Are all resource assumptions documented?

126. How do you know when you are finished?

127. Has adequate time for orientation & training of Desktop Application project staff been provided for in relation to technical nature of the application and the experience levels of Desktop Application project personnel?

128. Are agendas created for each meeting with meeting objectives, meeting topics, invitee list, and action items from past meetings?

2.3 Requirements Management Plan: Desktop Application

129. Is the user satisfied?

130. Did you avoid subjective, flowery or non-specific statements?

131. Will you use tracing to help understand the impact of a change in requirements?

132. Should you include sub-activities?

133. Who will perform the analysis?

134. What are you counting on?

135. If it exists, where is it housed?

136. Did you use declarative statements?

137. Could inaccurate or incomplete requirements in this Desktop Application project create a serious risk for the business?

138. How knowledgeable is the team in the proposed application area?

139. Which hardware or software, related to, or as outcome of the Desktop Application project is new to your organization?

140. Have stakeholders been instructed in the Change

Control process?

141. What are you trying to do?

142. Is any organizational data being used or stored?

143. Is the system software (non-operating system) new to the IT Desktop Application project team?

144. Business analysis scope?

145. In case of software development; Should you have a test for each code module?

146. How will the requirements become prioritized?

147. Is it new or replacing an existing business system or process?

148. What information regarding the Desktop Application project requirements will be reported?

2.4 Requirements Documentation: Desktop Application

149. What facilities must be supported by the system?

150. What is a show stopper in the requirements?

151. Are all functions required by the customer included?

152. Does your organization restrict technical alternatives?

153. How will requirements be documented and who signs off on them?

154. What will be the integration problems?

155. Can the requirements be checked?

156. What marketing channels do you want to use: e-mail, letter or sms?

157. How will the proposed Desktop Application project help?

158. How does the proposed Desktop Application project contribute to the overall objectives of your organization?

159. Is the origin of the requirement clearly stated?

160. Is new technology needed?

161. Consistency. are there any requirements conflicts?

162. How much testing do you need to do to prove that your system is safe?

163. Who is interacting with the system?

164. Can you check system requirements?

165. What is effective documentation?

166. How will they be documented / shared?

167. Is the requirement realistically testable?

168. What are the acceptance criteria?

2.5 Requirements Traceability Matrix: Desktop Application

169. Why use a WBS?

170. How small is small enough?

171. What percentage of Desktop Application projects are producing traceability matrices between requirements and other work products?

172. Describe the process for approving requirements so they can be added to the traceability matrix and Desktop Application project work can be performed. Will the Desktop Application project requirements become approved in writing?

173. How do you manage scope?

174. How will it affect the stakeholders personally in career?

175. Do you have a clear understanding of all subcontracts in place?

176. Will you use a Requirements Traceability Matrix?

177. What are the chronologies, contingencies, consequences, criteria?

178. Is there a requirements traceability process in place?

179. Why do you manage scope?

180. What is the WBS?

2.6 Project Scope Statement: Desktop Application

181. What actions will be taken to mitigate the risk?

182. Is an issue management process documented and filed?

183. Identify how your team and you will create the Desktop Application project scope statement and the work breakdown structure (WBS). Document how you will create the Desktop Application project scope statement and WBS, and make sure you answer the following questions: In defining Desktop Application project scope and the WBS, will you and your Desktop Application project team be using methods defined by your organization, methods defined by the Desktop Application project management office (PMO), or other methods?

184. Is there a Change Management Board?

185. Are the meetings set up to have assigned note takers that will add action/issues to the issue list?

186. Relevant - ask yourself can you get there; why are you doing this Desktop Application project?

187. Will all tasks resulting from issues be entered into the Desktop Application project Plan and tracked through the plan?

188. Elements that deal with providing the detail?

189. Is this process communicated to the customer and team members?

190. Will the Desktop Application project risks be managed according to the Desktop Application projects risk management process?

191. Is the Desktop Application project organization documented and on file?

192. Is the plan for Desktop Application project resources adequate?

193. Is the Desktop Application project sponsor function identified and defined?

194. Is there a process (test plans, inspections, reviews) defined for verifying outputs for each task?

195. Desktop Application project lead, team lead, solution architect?

196. What should you drop in order to add something new?

197. Are there issues that could affect the existing requirements for the result, service, or product if the scope changes?

198. Will you need a statement of work?

199. What is the product of this Desktop Application project?

2.7 Assumption and Constraint Log: Desktop Application

200. What do you audit?

201. Can you perform this task or activity in a more effective manner?

202. Do documented requirements exist for all critical components and areas, including technical, business, interfaces, performance, security and conversion requirements?

203. Are processes for release management of new development from coding and unit testing, to integration testing, to training, and production defined and followed?

204. Is the amount of effort justified by the anticipated value of forming a new process?

205. Can the requirements be traced to the appropriate components of the solution, as well as test scripts?

206. What strengths do you have?

207. How many Desktop Application project staff does this specific process affect?

208. When can log be discarded?

209. Is there adequate stakeholder participation for

the vetting of requirements definition, changes and management?

210. How relevant is this attribute to this Desktop Application project or audit?

211. Are best practices and metrics employed to identify issues, progress, performance, etc.?

212. Is the definition of the Desktop Application project scope clear; what needs to be accomplished?

213. Does a documented Desktop Application project organizational policy & plan (i.e. governance model) exist?

214. Were the system requirements formally reviewed prior to initiating the design phase?

215. Have Desktop Application project management standards and procedures been established and documented?

216. Is there documentation of system capability requirements, data requirements, environment requirements, security requirements, and computer and hardware requirements?

217. How can constraints be violated?

218. Have you eliminated all duplicative tasks or manual efforts, where appropriate?

219. Are there ways to reduce the time it takes to get something approved?

2.8 Work Breakdown Structure: Desktop Application

220. When do you stop?

221. How big is a work-package?

222. What has to be done?

223. How many levels?

224. Is it still viable?

225. Is the work breakdown structure (wbs) defined and is the scope of the Desktop Application project clear with assigned deliverable owners?

226. Is it a change in scope?

227. Where does it take place?

228. When does it have to be done?

229. How much detail?

230. How far down?

231. Why would you develop a Work Breakdown Structure?

232. How will you and your Desktop Application project team define the Desktop Application projects scope and work breakdown structure?

233. When would you develop a Work Breakdown Structure?

234. Who has to do it?

235. Can you make it?

2.9 WBS Dictionary: Desktop Application

236. Do work packages consist of discrete tasks which are adequately described?

237. Are procedures established to prevent changes to the contract budget base other than the already stated authorized by contractual action?

238. Are the bases and rates for allocating costs from each indirect pool to commercial work consistent with the already stated used to allocate corresponding costs to Government contracts?

239. Are retroactive changes to budgets for completed work specifically prohibited in an established procedure, and is this procedure adhered to?

240. Evaluate the performance of operating organizations?

241. Is cost and schedule performance measurement done in a consistent, systematic manner?

242. Are control accounts opened and closed based on the start and completion of work contained therein?

243. Do work packages reflect the actual way in which the work will be done and are they meaningful products or management-oriented subdivisions of a

higher level element of work?

244. Can the contractor substantiate work package and planning package budgets?

245. Is data disseminated to the contractors management timely, accurate, and usable?

246. Are records maintained to show how undistributed budgets are controlled?

247. Appropriate work authorization documents which subdivide the contractual effort and responsibilities, within functional organizations?

248. What is the end result of a work package?

249. Are the rates for allocating costs from each indirect cost pool to contracts updated as necessary to ensure a realistic monthly allocation of indirect costs without significant year-end adjustments?

250. Changes in the current direct and Desktop Application projected base?

251. Are current work performance indicators and goals relatable to original goals as modified by contractual changes, replanning, and reprogramming actions?

2.10 Schedule Management Plan: Desktop Application

252. Were stakeholders aware and supportive of the principles and practices of modern software estimation?

253. Are the Desktop Application project plans updated on a frequent basis?

254. Are action items captured and managed?

255. Are Desktop Application project team members committed fulltime?

256. Have adequate resources been provided by management to ensure Desktop Application project success?

257. Is there a Steering Committee in place?

258. Is quality monitored from the perspective of the customers needs and expectations?

259. Are updated Desktop Application project time & resource estimates reasonable based on the current Desktop Application project stage?

260. What will be the final cost of the Desktop Application project if status quo is maintained?

261. Can be realistically shortened (the duration of subsequent tasks)?

262. Are estimating assumptions and constraints captured?

263. Are target dates established for each milestone deliverable?

264. List all schedule constraints here. Must the Desktop Application project be complete by a specified date?

265. Is the steering committee active in Desktop Application project oversight?

266. Does the time Desktop Application projection include an amount for contingencies (time reserves)?

267. Are post milestone Desktop Application project reviews (PMPR) conducted with your organization at least once a year?

268. Goal: is the schedule feasible and at what cost?

269. Have all documents been archived in a Desktop Application project repository for each release?

270. Are issues raised, assessed, actioned, and resolved in a timely and efficient manner?

271. Which status reports are received per the Desktop Application project Plan?

2.11 Activity List: Desktop Application

272. What is your organizations history in doing similar activities?

273. Is infrastructure setup part of your Desktop Application project?

274. How detailed should a Desktop Application project get?

275. Are the required resources available or need to be acquired?

276. Who will perform the work?

277. The wbs is developed as part of a joint planning session. and how do you know that youhave done this right?

278. When will the work be performed?

279. What did not go as well?

280. What is the LF and LS for each activity?

281. Can you determine the activity that must finish, before this activity can start?

282. Is there anything planned that does not need to be here?

283. How difficult will it be to do specific activities on this Desktop Application project?

284. How should ongoing costs be monitored to try to keep the Desktop Application project within budget?

285. What are the critical bottleneck activities?

286. How will it be performed?

287. Where will it be performed?

288. What is the total time required to complete the Desktop Application project if no delays occur?

2.12 Activity Attributes: Desktop Application

289. How else could the items be grouped?

290. Why?

291. Does your organization of the data change its meaning?

292. Where else does it apply?

293. Do you feel very comfortable with your prediction?

294. Have you identified the Activity Leveling Priority code value on each activity?

295. Are the required resources available?

296. Has management defined a definite timeframe for the turnaround or Desktop Application project window?

297. What conclusions/generalizations can you draw from this?

298. Activity: fair or not fair?

299. Can you re-assign any activities to another resource to resolve an over-allocation?

300. How many days do you need to complete the

work scope with a limit of X number of resources?

301. Have constraints been applied to the start and finish milestones for the phases?

302. How difficult will it be to complete specific activities on this Desktop Application project?

303. How much activity detail is required?

304. How difficult will it be to do specific activities on this Desktop Application project?

305. Activity: what is Missing?

306. Activity: what is In the Bag?

2.13 Milestone List: Desktop Application

307. Can you derive how soon can the whole Desktop Application project finish?

308. Competitive advantages?

309. Identify critical paths (one or more) and which activities are on the critical path?

310. Legislative effects?

311. How soon can the activity start?

312. Describe your organizations strengths and core competencies. What factors will make your organization succeed?

313. Global influences?

314. Continuity, supply chain robustness?

315. Timescales, deadlines and pressures?

316. Effects on core activities, distraction?

317. What date will the task finish?

318. How late can the activity start?

319. Vital contracts and partners?

320. Usps (unique selling points)?

321. It is to be a narrative text providing the crucial aspects of your Desktop Application project proposal answering what, who, how, when and where?

322. Gaps in capabilities?

323. When will the Desktop Application project be complete?

324. What are your competitors vulnerabilities?

2.14 Network Diagram: Desktop Application

325. How difficult will it be to do specific activities on this Desktop Application project?

326. Why must you schedule milestones, such as reviews, throughout the Desktop Application project?

327. What must be completed before an activity can be started?

328. Can you calculate the confidence level?

329. What is the completion time?

330. What job or jobs follow it?

331. Will crashing x weeks return more in benefits than it costs?

332. If x is long, what would be the completion time if you break x into two parallel parts of y weeks and z weeks?

333. Review the logical flow of the network diagram. Take a look at which activities you have first and then sequence the activities. Do they make sense?

334. What is the lowest cost to complete this Desktop Application project in xx weeks?

335. Where do you schedule uncertainty time?

336. What are the tools?

337. What activities must occur simultaneously with this activity?

338. If the Desktop Application project network diagram cannot change and you have extra personnel resources, what is the BEST thing to do?

339. What activities must follow this activity?

340. Are you on time?

341. What job or jobs could run concurrently?

342. Where do schedules come from?

2.15 Activity Resource Requirements: Desktop Application

343. What is the Work Plan Standard?

344. When does monitoring begin?

345. What are constraints that you might find during the Human Resource Planning process?

346. Anything else?

347. How do you handle petty cash?

348. Do you use tools like decomposition and rolling-wave planning to produce the activity list and other outputs?

349. Are there unresolved issues that need to be addressed?

350. Organizational Applicability?

351. Other support in specific areas?

352. Why do you do that?

353. Which logical relationship does the PDM use most often?

354. How many signatures do you require on a check and does this match what is in your policy and procedures?

355. Time for overtime?

2.16 Resource Breakdown Structure: Desktop Application

356. What is the number one predictor of a groups productivity?

357. Which resource planning tool provides information on resource responsibility and accountability?

358. Who needs what information?

359. Why is this important?

360. What is each stakeholders desired outcome for the Desktop Application project?

361. What defines a successful Desktop Application project?

362. Why do you do it?

363. What is the primary purpose of the human resource plan?

364. Who will use the system?

365. What is the purpose of assigning and documenting responsibility?

366. Why time management?

367. Who is allowed to perform which functions?

368. What defines a successful Desktop Application project?

369. How can this help you with team building?

370. Any changes from stakeholders?

371. What is Desktop Application project communication management?

372. What is the difference between % Complete and % work?

373. What can you do to improve productivity?

2.17 Activity Duration Estimates: Desktop Application

374. Does the software appear easy to learn?

375. How can organizations use a weighted decision matrix to evaluate proposals as part of source selection?

376. How could you use each technique in your organization?

377. Is a formal written notice that the contract is complete provided to the seller?

378. How difficult will it be to do specific activities on this Desktop Application project?

379. Are updates on work results collected and used as inputs to the performance reporting process?

380. Is the work performed reviewed against contractual objectives?

381. Do an internet search on earning pmp certification. be sure to search for yahoo groups related to this topic. what are the options you found to help people prepare for the exam?

382. Given your research into similar classes and the work you think is required for this Desktop Application project, what assumptions, variables, or costs would you change from the information

provided above?

383. Are procedures followed to ensure information is available to stakeholders in a timely manner?

384. It under budget or over budget?

385. Is a work breakdown structure created to organize and to confirm the scope of each Desktop Application project?

386. Are operational definitions created to identify quality measurement criteria for specific activities?

387. Do Desktop Application project team members work in the same physical location to enhance team performance?

388. How difficult will it be to complete specific activities on this Desktop Application project?

389. Consider the common sources of risk on information technology Desktop Application projects and suggestions for managing them. Which suggestions do you find most useful?

390. Find an example of a contract for information technology services. Analyze the key features of the contract. What type of contract was used and why?

391. Will the new application negatively affect the current IT infrastructure?

392. Consider the examples of poor quality in information technology Desktop Application projects presented in the What Went Wrong?

2.18 Duration Estimating Worksheet: Desktop Application

393. Will the Desktop Application project collaborate with the local community and leverage resources?

394. Why estimate time and cost?

395. What is an Average Desktop Application project?

396. Is a construction detail attached (to aid in explanation)?

397. When, then?

398. How should ongoing costs be monitored to try to keep the Desktop Application project within budget?

399. What work will be included in the Desktop Application project?

400. Define the work as completely as possible. What work will be included in the Desktop Application project?

401. Do any colleagues have experience with your organization and/or RFPs?

402. Done before proceeding with this activity or what can be done concurrently?

403. What utility impacts are there?

404. Value pocket identification & quantification what are value pockets?

405. What questions do you have?

406. What is the total time required to complete the Desktop Application project if no delays occur?

407. How can the Desktop Application project be displayed graphically to better visualize the activities?

408. Small or large Desktop Application project?

409. What is next?

410. When does your organization expect to be able to complete it?

411. Why estimate costs?

2.19 Project Schedule: Desktop Application

412. How do you use schedules?

413. If there are any qualifying green components to this Desktop Application project, what portion of the total Desktop Application project cost is green?

414. How can slack be negative?

415. What does that mean?

416. Is the Desktop Application project schedule available for all Desktop Application project team members to review?

417. Eliminate unnecessary activities. Are there activities that came from a template or previous Desktop Application project that are not applicable on this phase of this Desktop Application project?

418. Why is software Desktop Application project disaster so common?

419. To what degree is do you feel the entire team was committed to the Desktop Application project schedule?

420. What is the most mis-scheduled part of process?

421. Is the structure for tracking the Desktop Application project schedule well defined and

assigned to a specific individual?

422. Are there activities that came from a template or previous Desktop Application project that are not applicable on this phase of this Desktop Application project?

423. How do you manage Desktop Application project Risk?

424. Was the Desktop Application project schedule reviewed by all stakeholders and formally accepted?

425. Your best shot for providing estimations how complex/how much work does the activity require?

426. How much slack is available in the Desktop Application project?

427. How effectively were issues able to be resolved without impacting the Desktop Application project Schedule or Budget?

2.20 Cost Management Plan: Desktop Application

428. Contingency – how will cost contingency be administered?

429. Eac -estimate at completion, what is the total job expected to cost?

430. Is there an approved case?

431. Have reserves been created to address risks?

432. Change types and category – What are the types of changes and what are the techniques to report and control changes?

433. Is Desktop Application project status reviewed with the steering and executive teams at appropriate intervals?

434. Is your organization certified as a supplier, wholesaler and/or regular dealer?

435. Are any non-compliance issues that exist due to State practices communicated to your organization?

436. Are risk triggers captured?

437. Is your organization certified as a supplier, wholesaler, regular dealer, or manufacturer of corresponding products/supplies?

438. Has your organization readiness assessment been conducted?

439. Are staff skills known and available for each task?

440. Risk Analysis?

441. Are actuals compared against estimates to analyze and correct variances?

442. Does a documented Desktop Application project organizational policy & plan (i.e. governance model) exist?

443. Does the Desktop Application project have a formal Desktop Application project Charter?

444. Does the business case include how the Desktop Application project aligns with your organizations strategic goals & objectives?

445. Have Desktop Application project management standards and procedures been identified / established and documented?

2.21 Activity Cost Estimates: Desktop Application

446. Maintenance Reserve?

447. Can you change your activities?

448. What defines a successful Desktop Application project?

449. When do you enter into PPM?

450. What is the activity recast of the budget?

451. What is the activity inventory?

452. Based on your Desktop Application project communication management plan, what worked well?

453. What skill level is required to do the job?

454. What is Desktop Application project cost management?

455. How do you fund change orders?

456. What do you want to know about the stay to know if costs were inappropriately high or low?

457. Does the estimator estimate by task or by person?

458. Did the Desktop Application project team have the right skills?

459. Was it performed on time?

460. What is included in indirect cost being allocated?

461. Is costing method consistent with study goals?

462. If you are asked to lower your estimate because the price is too high, what are your options?

463. How many activities should you have?

2.22 Cost Estimating Worksheet: Desktop Application

464. What happens to any remaining funds not used?

465. Can a trend be established from historical performance data on the selected measure and are the criteria for using trend analysis or forecasting methods met?

466. What can be included?

467. Will the Desktop Application project collaborate with the local community and leverage resources?

468. Who is best positioned to know and assist in identifying corresponding factors?

469. Is the Desktop Application project responsive to community need?

470. What costs are to be estimated?

471. What is the estimated labor cost today based upon this information?

472. What additional Desktop Application project(s) could be initiated as a result of this Desktop Application project?

473. Ask: are others positioned to know, are others credible, and will others cooperate?

474. Identify the timeframe necessary to monitor progress and collect data to determine how the selected measure has changed?

475. What info is needed?

476. Does the Desktop Application project provide innovative ways for stakeholders to overcome obstacles or deliver better outcomes?

477. What is the purpose of estimating?

478. What will others want?

479. Is it feasible to establish a control group arrangement?

480. How will the results be shared and to whom?

2.23 Cost Baseline: Desktop Application

481. Has the documentation relating to operation and maintenance of the product(s) or service(s) been delivered to, and accepted by, operations management?

482. What can go wrong?

483. What is the consequence?

484. Has the Desktop Application project (or Desktop Application project phase) been evaluated against each objective established in the product description and Integrated Desktop Application project Plan?

485. Has operations management formally accepted responsibility for operating and maintaining the product(s) or service(s) delivered by the Desktop Application project?

486. How will cost estimates be used?

487. What deliverables come first?

488. Where do changes come from?

489. Is request in line with priorities?

490. Have all approved changes to the schedule baseline been identified and impact on the Desktop Application project documented?

491. What is your organizations history in doing similar tasks?

492. If you sold 10x widgets on a day, what would the affect on profits be?

493. Is the requested change request a result of changes in other Desktop Application project(s)?

494. Does the suggested change request seem to represent a necessary enhancement to the product?

495. Vac -variance at completion, how much over/ under budget do you expect to be?

496. What is it ?

497. Have all approved changes to the Desktop Application project requirement been identified and impact on the performance, cost, and schedule baselines documented?

498. How likely is it to go wrong?

499. Is the cr within Desktop Application project scope?

2.24 Quality Management Plan: Desktop Application

500. Where do you focus?

501. How are your organizations compensation and recognition approaches and the performance management system used to reinforce high performance?

502. Do you keep back-up copies of any data?

503. What data do you gather/use/compile?

504. Are there trends or hot spots?

505. Who gets results of work?

506. How is staff informed of proper reporting methods?

507. How are records kept in the office?

508. How will you know that a change is actually an improvement?

509. Does the Desktop Application project have a formal Desktop Application project Plan?

510. How does your organization maintain a safe and healthy work environment?

511. Who needs a qmp?

512. Who is responsible?

513. What is positive about the current process?

514. After observing execution of process, is it in compliance with the documented Plan?

515. Are requirements management tracking tools and procedures in place?

516. Are there standards for code development?

517. Have Desktop Application project management standards and procedures been established and documented?

518. How is staff trained on the recording of field notes?

2.25 Quality Metrics: Desktop Application

519. How do you communicate results and findings to upper management?

520. Are quality metrics defined?

521. Where is quality now?

522. Was review conducted per standard protocols?

523. What about still open problems?

524. What forces exist that would cause them to change?

525. Why is now the time for quality metrics?

526. What does this tell us?

527. When is the security analysis testing complete?

528. What is the benchmark?

529. What group is empowered to define quality requirements?

530. The metrics–what is being considered?

531. How should customers provide input?

532. Has trace of defects been initiated?

533. Are there any open risk issues?

534. Is quality culture a competitive advantage?

535. What happens if you get an abnormal result?

536. Is there a set of procedures to capture, analyze and act on quality metrics?

537. What percentage are outcome-based?

2.26 Process Improvement Plan: Desktop Application

538. To elicit goal statements, do you ask a question such as, What do you want to achieve?

539. What lessons have you learned so far?

540. Everyone agrees on what process improvement is, right?

541. Does your process ensure quality?

542. Has a process guide to collect the data been developed?

543. Why do you want to achieve the goal?

544. Where are you now?

545. Are you following the quality standards?

546. Have storage and access mechanisms and procedures been determined?

547. Who should prepare the process improvement action plan?

548. Has the time line required to move measurement results from the points of collection to databases or users been established?

549. Have the supporting tools been developed or

acquired?

550. Modeling current processes is great, and will you ever see a return on that investment?

551. Are you making progress on your improvement plan?

552. Are there forms and procedures to collect and record the data?

553. What personnel are the change agents for your initiative?

554. How do you measure?

555. Does explicit definition of the measures exist?

556. Are you making progress on the goals?

2.27 Responsibility Assignment Matrix: Desktop Application

557. How do you assist them to be as productive as possible?

558. Is all contract work included in the CWBS?

559. Identify potential or actual overruns and underruns?

560. Undistributed budgets, if any?

561. Does the Desktop Application project need to be analyzed further to uncover additional responsibilities?

562. Wbs elements contractually specified for reporting of status (lowest level only)?

563. What do you do when people do not respond?

564. What does wbs accomplish?

565. The anticipated business volume?

566. All cwbs elements specified for external reporting?

567. What happens when others get pulled for higher priority Desktop Application projects?

568. Are management actions taken to reduce

indirect costs when there are significant adverse variances?

569. Time-phased control account budgets?

570. Are all authorized tasks assigned to identified organizational elements?

571. Are indirect costs accumulated for comparison with the corresponding budgets?

572. Does the contractors system provide unit or lot costs when applicable?

573. Which Desktop Application project management knowledge area is least mature?

2.28 Roles and Responsibilities: Desktop Application

574. Are governance roles and responsibilities documented?

575. What are your major roles and responsibilities in the area of performance measurement and assessment?

576. Who is responsible for each task?

577. What should you do now to ensure that you are exceeding expectations and excelling in your current position?

578. Do you take the time to clearly define roles and responsibilities on Desktop Application project tasks?

579. Once the responsibilities are defined for the Desktop Application project, have the deliverables, roles and responsibilities been clearly communicated to every participant?

580. Are Desktop Application project team roles and responsibilities identified and documented?

581. How well did the Desktop Application project Team understand the expectations of specific roles and responsibilities?

582. Is there a training program in place for stakeholders covering expectations, roles and

responsibilities and any addition knowledge others need to be good stakeholders?

583. Be specific; avoid generalities. Thank you and great work alone are insufficient. What exactly do you appreciate and why?

584. What areas would you highlight for changes or improvements?

585. What should you highlight for improvement?

586. Is feedback clearly communicated and non-judgmental?

587. What is working well?

588. Are your policies supportive of a culture of quality data?

589. What expectations were NOT met?

590. Was the expectation clearly communicated?

591. What expectations were met?

2.29 Human Resource Management Plan: Desktop Application

592. Is Desktop Application project work proceeding in accordance with the original Desktop Application project schedule?

593. Were Desktop Application project team members involved in detailed estimating and scheduling?

594. Have activity relationships and interdependencies within tasks been adequately identified?

595. Who needs training?

596. What were things that you did very well and want to do the same again on the next Desktop Application project?

597. Are assumptions being identified, recorded, analyzed, qualified and closed?

598. Have all documents been archived in a Desktop Application project repository for each release?

599. Are the quality tools and methods identified in the Quality Plan appropriate to the Desktop Application project?

600. Has a provision been made to reassess Desktop Application project risks at various Desktop Application project stages?

601. Is there a formal set of procedures supporting Stakeholder Management?

602. Personnel with expertise?

603. Does the resource management plan include a personnel development plan?

604. Have the key functions and capabilities been defined and assigned to each release or iteration?

605. Were stakeholders aware and supportive of the principles and practices of modern cost estimation?

606. Has a structured approach been used to break work effort into manageable components (WBS)?

607. Pareto diagrams, statistical sampling, flow charting or trend analysis used quality monitoring?

608. Is your organization human?

2.30 Communications Management Plan: Desktop Application

609. How will the person responsible for executing the communication item be notified?

610. Timing: when do the effects of the communication take place?

611. Why manage stakeholders?

612. Do you feel more overwhelmed by stakeholders?

613. Do you prepare stakeholder engagement plans?

614. Who will use or be affected by the result of a Desktop Application project?

615. Who needs to know and how much?

616. Who are the members of the governing body?

617. Which team member will work with each stakeholder?

618. Are stakeholders internal or external?

619. Who did you turn to if you had questions?

620. Which stakeholders can influence others?

621. Are there common objectives between the team and the stakeholder?

622. Conflict resolution -which method when?

623. What is the political influence?

624. What is the stakeholders level of authority?

625. Are the stakeholders getting the information others need, are others consulted, are concerns addressed?

626. Who to learn from?

627. How often do you engage with stakeholders?

628. Is the stakeholder role recognized by your organization?

2.31 Risk Management Plan: Desktop Application

629. Are the reports useful and easy to read?

630. Was an original risk assessment/risk management plan completed?

631. Technology risk: is the Desktop Application project technically feasible?

632. Does the Desktop Application project have the authority and ability to avoid the risk?

633. What risks are necessary to achieve success?

634. What can you do to minimize the impact if it does?

635. How is risk response planning performed?

636. Premium on reliability of product?

637. Where do risks appear in the business phases?

638. How is the audit profession changing?

639. Workarounds are determined during which step of risk management?

640. Does the software engineering team have the right mix of skills?

641. Is the number of people on the Desktop Application project team adequate to do the job?

642. Are testing tools available and suitable?

643. Why do you want risk management?

644. Are Desktop Application project requirements stable?

645. What are the chances the event will occur?

646. My Desktop Application project leader has suddenly left your organization, what do you do?

647. What are the cost, schedule and resource impacts of avoiding the risk?

648. What things might go wrong?

2.32 Risk Register: Desktop Application

649. Having taken action, how did the responses effect change, and where is the Desktop Application project now?

650. What should you do now?

651. Are there other alternative controls that could be implemented?

652. What could prevent you delivering on the strategic program objectives and what is being done to mitigate corresponding issues?

653. What action, if any, has been taken to respond to the risk?

654. User involvement: do you have the right users?

655. Severity Prediction?

656. What are the assumptions and current status that support the assessment of the risk?

657. Methodology: how will risk management be performed on this Desktop Application project?

658. Does the evidence highlight any areas to advance opportunities or foster good relations. If yes what steps will be taken?

659. Technology risk -is the Desktop Application project technically feasible?

660. Which key risks have ineffective responses or outstanding improvement actions?

661. Manageability – have mitigations to the risk been identified?

662. Amongst the action plans and recommendations that you have to introduce are there some that could stop or delay the overall program?

663. What will be done?

664. What are your key risks/show istoppers and what is being done to manage them?

665. What evidence do you have to justify the likelihood score of the risk (audit, incident report, claim, complaints, inspection, internal review)?

666. Have other controls and solutions been implemented in other services which could be applied as an alternative to additional funding?

667. How are risks identified?

668. Risk documentation: what reporting formats and processes will be used for risk management activities?

2.33 Probability and Impact Assessment: Desktop Application

669. Are people attending meetings and doing work?

670. Are tools for analysis and design available?

671. Is a software Desktop Application project management tool available?

672. How realistic is the timing of introduction?

673. How would you assess the risk management process in the Desktop Application project?

674. Have top software and customer managers formally committed to support the Desktop Application project?

675. What are the risks involved in appointing external agencies to manage the Desktop Application project?

676. Do you use diagramming techniques to show cause and effect?

677. What risks does your organization have if the Desktop Application projects fail to meet deadline?

678. What is the level of experience available with your organization?

679. Is the process supported by tools?

680. Supply/demand Desktop Application projections and trends; what are the levels of accuracy?

681. Is the technology to be built new to your organization?

682. How well is the risk understood?

683. Do you manage the process through use of metrics?

684. How completely has the customer been identified?

685. What are the industrial relations prevailing in your organization?

686. How do risks change during a Desktop Application project life cycle?

687. Risk categorization -which of your categories has more risk than others?

2.34 Probability and Impact Matrix: Desktop Application

688. Does the Desktop Application project team have experience with the technology to be implemented?

689. What will be the likely incidence of conflict with neighboring Desktop Application projects?

690. What action do you usually take against risks?

691. During Desktop Application project executing, a team member identifies a risk that is not in the risk register. What should you do?

692. What needs to be DONE?

693. What new technologies are being explored in the same area?

694. Are you on schedule?

695. Economic to take on the Desktop Application project?

696. What can you do about it?

697. Lay ground work for future returns?

698. Which is an input to the risk management process?

699. Is the customer technically sophisticated in the

product area?

700. Is the customer willing to participate in reviews?

701. What can you use the analyzed risks for?

702. Can it be enlarged by drawing people from other areas of your organization?

703. Who should be notified of the occurrence of each of the risk indicators?

704. What action would you take to the identified risks in the Desktop Application project?

705. Are compilers and code generators available and suitable for the product to be built?

706. Are enough people available?

2.35 Risk Data Sheet: Desktop Application

707. What are you trying to achieve (Objectives)?

708. What is the chance that it will happen?

709. What is the likelihood of it happening?

710. Potential for recurrence?

711. Whom do you serve (customers)?

712. Do effective diagnostic tests exist?

713. What actions can be taken to eliminate or remove risk?

714. What can happen?

715. Will revised controls lead to tolerable risk levels?

716. What do people affected think about the need for, and practicality of preventive measures?

717. Are new hazards created?

718. What are you here for (Mission)?

719. What are the main opportunities available to you that you should grab while you can?

720. What were the Causes that contributed?

721. How reliable is the data source?

722. What do you know?

723. What are the main threats to your existence?

724. How can hazards be reduced?

725. What are you weak at and therefore need to do better?

726. How can it happen?

2.36 Procurement Management Plan: Desktop Application

727. Have the procedures for identifying budget variances been followed?

728. What is a Desktop Application project Management Plan?

729. Have key stakeholders been identified?

730. Are written status reports provided on a designated frequent basis?

731. Is there a procurement management plan in place?

732. Published materials?

733. If independent estimates will be needed as evaluation criteria, who will prepare them and when?

734. Are enough systems & user personnel assigned to the Desktop Application project?

735. Is the steering committee active in Desktop Application project oversight?

736. Has the scope management document been updated and distributed to help prevent scope creep?

737. Are tasks tracked by hours?

738. Are there checklists created to determine if all quality processes are followed?

739. Do all stakeholders know how to access the PM repository and where to find the Desktop Application project documentation?

740. Are the people assigned to the Desktop Application project sufficiently qualified?

741. Are post milestone Desktop Application project reviews (PMPR) conducted with your organization at least once a year?

2.37 Source Selection Criteria: Desktop Application

742. Has all proposal data been loaded?

743. Is this a cost contract?

744. What is price analysis and when should it be performed?

745. Who is entitled to a debriefing?

746. What evidence should be provided regarding proposal evaluations?

747. Are there any specific considerations that precludes offers from being selected as the awardee?

748. What past performance information should be requested?

749. Do proposed hours support content and schedule?

750. What should be the contracting officers strategy?

751. What aspects should the contracting officer brief the Desktop Application project on prior to evaluation of proposals?

752. What are the most critical evaluation criteria that prove to be tiebreakers in the evaluation of proposals?

753. Are there any common areas of weaknesses or deficiencies in the proposals in the competitive range?

754. Does your documentation identify why the team concurs or differs with reported performance from past performance report (CPARs, questionnaire responses, etc.)?

755. What should a DRFP include?

756. Are evaluators ready to begin this task?

757. How will you decide an evaluators write up is sufficient?

758. What is the effect of the debriefing schedule on potential protests?

759. Team leads: what is your process for assigning ratings?

760. Do you have designated specific forms or worksheets?

761. When is it appropriate to issue a DRFP?

2.38 Stakeholder Management Plan: Desktop Application

762. Are decisions captured in a decisions log?

763. Is a payment system in place with proper reviews and approvals?

764. Are the schedule estimates reasonable given the Desktop Application project?

765. Who is accountable for the achievement of the targeted outcome(s) and reports on the progress towards the target?

766. Do Desktop Application project managers participating in the Desktop Application project know the Desktop Application projects true status first hand?

767. Have stakeholder accountabilities & responsibilities been clearly defined?

768. Are vendor invoices audited for accuracy before payment?

769. Is stakeholder involvement adequate?

770. Are post milestone Desktop Application project reviews (PMPR) conducted with your organization at least once a year?

771. Does the Desktop Application project have a

formal Desktop Application project Charter?

772. Has a capability assessment been conducted?

773. Do you know what your customers expectations are regarding this process?

774. Are communication systems proposed compatible with staff skills and experience?

775. Who would sign off on the charter?

776. What has to be purchased?

777. Does the Desktop Application project have a Statement of Work?

2.39 Change Management Plan: Desktop Application

778. How much Desktop Application project management is needed?

779. Is there a support model for this application and are the details available for distribution?

780. What work practices will be affected?

781. Readiness -what is a successful end state?

782. How many people are required in each of the roles?

783. What prerequisite knowledge do corresponding groups need?

784. Who will do the training?

785. What are the dependencies?

786. What are the major changes to processes?

787. What is the worst thing that can happen if you communicate information?

788. Has the target training audience been identified and nominated?

789. What prerequisite knowledge or training is required?

790. What is going to be done differently?

791. What is the worst thing that can happen if you chose not to communicate this information?

792. Has an information & communications plan been developed?

793. Do the proposed users have access to the appropriate documentation?

794. Do there need to be new channels developed?

795. What relationships will change?

796. What tasks are needed?

797. Have the business unit contacts been briefed by the Desktop Application project team?

3.0 Executing Process Group: Desktop Application

798. What are the main types of goods and services being outsourced?

799. How well did the team follow the chosen processes?

800. Specific - is the objective clear in terms of what, how, when, and where the situation will be changed?

801. Will outside resources be needed to help?

802. How can software assist in procuring goods and services?

803. Why do you need a good WBS to use Desktop Application project management software?

804. Is the Desktop Application project making progress in helping to achieve the set results?

805. If a risk event occurs, what will you do?

806. Are the necessary foundations in place to ensure the sustainability of the results of the programme?

807. How will you avoid scope creep?

808. What were things that you need to improve?

809. Do your results resemble a normal distribution?

810. Will a new application be developed using existing hardware, software, and networks?

811. What were things that you did well, and could improve, and how?

812. Is the program supported by national and/or local organizations?

813. Does software appear easy to learn?

814. Will additional funds be needed for hardware or software?

815. What factors are contributing to progress or delay in the achievement of products and results?

816. Just how important is your work to the overall success of the Desktop Application project?

817. Do the products created live up to the necessary quality?

3.1 Team Member Status Report: Desktop Application

818. Do you have an Enterprise Desktop Application project Management Office (EPMO)?

819. What specific interest groups do you have in place?

820. How can you make it practical?

821. How much risk is involved?

822. How will resource planning be done?

823. Why is it to be done?

824. How does this product, good, or service meet the needs of the Desktop Application project and your organization as a whole?

825. Does the product, good, or service already exist within your organization?

826. Are the products of your organizations Desktop Application projects meeting customers objectives?

827. Will the staff do training or is that done by a third party?

828. What is to be done?

829. The problem with Reward & Recognition

Programs is that the truly deserving people all too often get left out. How can you make it practical?

830. Are your organizations Desktop Application projects more successful over time?

831. Is there evidence that staff is taking a more professional approach toward management of your organizations Desktop Application projects?

832. Are the attitudes of staff regarding Desktop Application project work improving?

833. Does your organization have the means (staff, money, contract, etc.) to produce or to acquire the product, good, or service?

834. How it is to be done?

835. When a teams productivity and success depend on collaboration and the efficient flow of information, what generally fails them?

836. Does every department have to have a Desktop Application project Manager on staff?

3.2 Change Request: Desktop Application

837. Screen shots or attachments included in a Change Request?

838. Which requirements attributes affect the risk to reliability the most?

839. How well do experienced software developers predict software change?

840. Who has responsibility for approving and ranking changes?

841. Should staff call into the helpdesk or go to the website?

842. How are changes graded and who is responsible for the rating?

843. Should a more thorough impact analysis be conducted?

844. Change request coordination ?

845. Who can suggest changes?

846. How many lines of code must be changed to implement the change?

847. Describe how modifications, enhancements, defects and/or deficiencies shall be notified (e.g.

Problem Reports, Change Requests etc) and managed. Detail warranty and/or maintenance periods?

848. Who needs to approve change requests?

849. Why control change across the life cycle?

850. Who is included in the change control team?

851. What are the basic mechanics of the Change Advisory Board (CAB)?

852. Has the change been highlighted and documented in the CSCI?

853. How is quality being addressed on the Desktop Application project?

854. Are change requests logged and managed?

3.3 Change Log: Desktop Application

855. How does this change affect the timeline of the schedule?

856. Is the change request within Desktop Application project scope?

857. When was the request approved?

858. Does the suggested change request represent a desired enhancement to the products functionality?

859. When was the request submitted?

860. Is the requested change request a result of changes in other Desktop Application project(s)?

861. Is the submitted change a new change or a modification of a previously approved change?

862. Is this a mandatory replacement?

863. How does this change affect scope?

864. How does this relate to the standards developed for specific business processes?

865. Who initiated the change request?

866. Will the Desktop Application project fail if the change request is not executed?

867. Is the change request open, closed or pending?

868. Do the described changes impact on the integrity or security of the system?

869. Is the change backward compatible without limitations?

3.4 Decision Log: Desktop Application

870. Do strategies and tactics aimed at less than full control reduce the costs of management or simply shift the cost burden?

871. Adversarial environment. is your opponent open to a non-traditional workflow, or will it likely challenge anything you do?

872. Meeting purpose; why does this team meet?

873. Who will be given a copy of this document and where will it be kept?

874. How do you know when you are achieving it?

875. How consolidated and comprehensive a story can you tell by capturing currently available incident data in a central location and through a log of key decisions during an incident?

876. What is the line where eDiscovery ends and document review begins?

877. How does the use a Decision Support System influence the strategies/tactics or costs?

878. What alternatives/risks were considered?

879. Linked to original objective?

880. What is the average size of your matters in an applicable measurement?

881. Behaviors; what are guidelines that the team has identified that will assist them with getting the most out of team meetings?

882. How do you define success?

883. Who is the decisionmaker?

884. What makes you different or better than others companies selling the same thing?

885. How does an increasing emphasis on cost containment influence the strategies and tactics used?

886. What are the cost implications?

887. Is your opponent open to a non-traditional workflow, or will it likely challenge anything you do?

888. Decision-making process; how will the team make decisions?

889. How effective is maintaining the log at facilitating organizational learning?

3.5 Quality Audit: Desktop Application

890. How does your organization know that its systems for assisting staff with career planning and employment placements are appropriately effective and constructive?

891. Health and safety arrangements; stress management workshops. How does your organization know that it provides a safe and healthy environment?

892. Are salvageable and salvaged medical devices stored in a manner to prevent damage and/or contamination?

893. How does your organization know that its system for commercializing research outputs is appropriately effective and constructive?

894. For each device to be reconditioned, are device specifications, such as appropriate engineering drawings, component specifications and software specifications, maintained?

895. How does your organization know that its quality of teaching is appropriately effective and constructive?

896. What are your supplier audits?

897. How does your organization know that its information technology system is serving its needs as

effectively and constructively as is appropriate?

898. Are people allowed to contribute ideas?

899. Quality is about improvement and accountability. The immediate questions that arise out of that statement are: (i) improvement on what, and (ii) accountable to whom?

900. How does your organization know that its staff financial services are appropriately effective and constructive?

901. How does your organization know that its system for managing intellectual property issues is appropriately effective, constructive and fair?

902. Is there any content that may be legally actionable?

903. How does your organization know that its staff support services planning and management systems are appropriately effective and constructive?

904. How does your organization know that its system for governing staff behaviour is appropriately effective and constructive?

905. Is there a risk that information provided by management may not always be reliable?

906. How does your organization know that its research programs are appropriately effective and constructive?

907. Have the risks associated with the intentions

been identified, analyzed and appropriate responses developed?

908. Statements of intent remain exactly that until they are put into effect. The next step is to deploy the already stated intentions. In other words, do the plans happen in reality?

909. How does your organization know that its policy management system is appropriately effective and constructive?

3.6 Team Directory: Desktop Application

910. Process decisions: do job conditions warrant additional actions to collect job information and document on-site activity?

911. What needs to be communicated?

912. How do unidentified risks impact the outcome of the Desktop Application project?

913. How will the team handle changes?

914. Days from the time the issue is identified?

915. When will you produce deliverables?

916. Process decisions: are there any statutory or regulatory issues relevant to the timely execution of work?

917. Why is the work necessary?

918. How and in what format should information be presented?

919. Contract requirements complied with?

920. How does the team resolve conflicts and ensure tasks are completed?

921. Timing: when do the effects of communication

take place?

922. Decisions: is the most suitable form of contract being used?

923. Who should receive information (all stakeholders)?

924. Decisions: what could be done better to improve the quality of the constructed product?

925. Does a Desktop Application project team directory list all resources assigned to the Desktop Application project?

926. Process decisions: are contractors adequately prosecuting the work?

927. Who will write the meeting minutes and distribute?

928. Who will talk to the customer?

929. When does information need to be distributed?

3.7 Team Operating Agreement: Desktop Application

930. Do you leverage technology engagement tools group chat, polls, screen sharing, etc.?

931. Do you begin with a question to engage everyone?

932. Do you upload presentation materials in advance and test the technology?

933. What are the boundaries (organizational or geographic) within which you operate?

934. What is a Virtual Team?

935. The method to be used in the decision making process; Will it be consensus, majority rule, or the supervisor having the final say?

936. Reimbursements: how will the team members be reimbursed for expenses and time commitments?

937. Did you prepare participants for the next meeting?

938. Are there more than two functional areas represented by your team?

939. Did you recap the meeting purpose, time, and expectations?

940. How will you divide work equitably?

941. Did you delegate tasks such as taking meeting minutes, presenting a topic and soliciting input?

942. What resources can be provided for the team in terms of equipment, space, time for training, protected time and space for meetings, and travel allowances?

943. Do you determine the meeting length and time of day?

944. Communication protocols: how will the team communicate?

945. Do you ensure that all participants know how to use the required technology?

946. What is group supervision?

947. Is compensation based on team and individual performance?

948. What is the number of cases currently teamed?

949. Methodologies: how will key team processes be implemented, such as training, research, work deliverable production, review and approval processes, knowledge management, and meeting procedures?

3.8 Team Performance Assessment: Desktop Application

950. How hard do you try to make a good selection?

951. To what degree does the teams purpose contain themes that are particularly meaningful and memorable?

952. To what degree do team members feel that the purpose of the team is important, if not exciting?

953. Lack of method variance in self-reported affect and perceptions at work: Reality or artifact?

954. Is there a particular method of data analysis that you would recommend as a means of demonstrating that method variance is not of great concern for a given dataset?

955. To what degree does the teams approach to its work allow for modification and improvement over time?

956. Do you give group members authority to make at least some important decisions?

957. To what degree can the team measure progress against specific goals?

958. What makes opportunities more or less obvious?

959. To what degree do team members understand

one anothers roles and skills?

960. What structural changes have you made or are you preparing to make?

961. To what degree are sub-teams possible or necessary?

962. Which situations call for a more extreme type of adaptiveness in which team members actually re-define roles?

963. To what degree does the teams work approach provide opportunity for members to engage in results-based evaluation?

964. Individual task proficiency and team process behavior: what is important for team functioning?

965. How do you keep key people outside the group informed about its accomplishments?

966. Do you promptly inform members about major developments that may affect them?

967. What do you think is the most constructive thing that could be done now to resolve considerations and disputes about method variance?

968. How do you encourage members to learn from each other?

969. How much interpersonal friction is there in your team?

3.9 Team Member Performance Assessment: Desktop Application

970. How does your team work together?

971. To what degree can team members frequently and easily communicate with one another?

972. How accurately is your plan implemented?

973. What instructional strategies were developed/ incorporated (e.g., direct instruction, indirect instruction, experiential learning, independent study, interactive instruction)?

974. What evidence supports your decision-making?

975. To what degree do all members feel responsible for all agreed-upon measures?

976. To what degree do team members frequently explore the teams purpose and its implications?

977. How are performance measures and associated incentives developed?

978. What are they responsible for?

979. Are the draft goals SMART ?

980. What evaluation results did you have?

981. What tools are available to determine whether

all contract functional and compliance areas of performance objectives, measures, and incentives have been met?

982. How is assessment information achieved, stored?

983. To what degree does the team possess adequate membership to achieve its ends?

984. Why do performance reviews?

985. How often should assessments be conducted?

986. To what degree do team members articulate the teams work approach?

987. Does the rater (supervisor) have to wait for the interim or final performance assessment review to tell an employee that the employees performance is unsatisfactory?

3.10 Issue Log: Desktop Application

988. Are you constantly rushing from meeting to meeting?

989. What approaches do you use?

990. Who is involved as you identify stakeholders?

991. In classifying stakeholders, which approach to do so are you using?

992. Who have you worked with in past, similar initiatives?

993. How much time does it take to do it?

994. Is access to the Issue Log controlled?

995. How is this initiative related to other portfolios, programs, or Desktop Application projects?

996. What are the stakeholders interrelationships?

997. What is a Stakeholder?

998. Do you feel a register helps?

999. Is the issue log kept in a safe place?

1000. Why not more evaluators?

1001. How were past initiatives successful?

1002. Why do you manage human resources?

1003. What would have to change?

1004. Who were proponents/opponents?

4.0 Monitoring and Controlling Process Group: Desktop Application

1005. What areas does the group agree are the biggest success on the Desktop Application project?

1006. Are there areas that need improvement?

1007. If action is called for, what form should it take?

1008. Is the program in place as intended?

1009. How is Agile Desktop Application project Management done?

1010. Do clients benefit (change) from the services?

1011. Is there sufficient time allotted between the general system design and the detailed system design phases?

1012. Based on your Desktop Application project communication management plan, what worked well?

1013. What communication items need improvement?

1014. What departments are involved in its daily operation?

1015. What will you do to minimize the impact should a risk event occur?

1016. What kinds of things in particular are you looking for data on?

1017. What is the timeline for the Desktop Application project?

1018. Do the partners have sufficient financial capacity to keep up the benefits produced by the programme?

1019. What is the expected monetary value of the Desktop Application project?

1020. Overall, how does the program function to serve the clients?

4.1 Project Performance Report: Desktop Application

1021. To what degree do team members agree with the goals, relative importance, and the ways in which achievement will be measured?

1022. To what degree do the goals specify concrete team work products?

1023. To what degree does the formal organization make use of individual resources and meet individual needs?

1024. To what degree will the approach capitalize on and enhance the skills of all team members in a manner that takes into consideration other demands on members of the team?

1025. To what degree is there a sense that only the team can succeed?

1026. To what degree are the demands of the task compatible with and converge with the relationships of the informal organization?

1027. To what degree are the goals ambitious?

1028. To what degree will new and supplemental skills be introduced as the need is recognized?

1029. How can Desktop Application project sustainability be maintained?

1030. What is the degree to which rules govern information exchange between individuals within your organization?

1031. To what degree does the funding match the requirement?

1032. To what degree are the goals realistic?

1033. What is in it for you?

1034. To what degree do members articulate the goals beyond the team membership?

1035. To what degree are the members clear on what they are individually responsible for and what they are jointly responsible for?

1036. To what degree will the team ensure that all members equitably share the work essential to the success of the team?

1037. How will procurement be coordinated with other Desktop Application project aspects, such as scheduling and performance reporting?

4.2 Variance Analysis: Desktop Application

1038. Are the wbs and organizational levels for application of the Desktop Application projected overhead costs identified?

1039. Are data elements reconcilable between internal summary reports and reports forwarded to the stakeholders?

1040. Did an existing competitor change strategy?

1041. Is budgeted cost for work performed calculated in a manner consistent with the way work is planned?

1042. Are overhead cost budgets established for each department which has authority to incur overhead costs?

1043. Historical experience?

1044. Did a new competitor enter the market?

1045. What is the budgeted cost for work scheduled?

1046. What is the expected future profitability of each customer?

1047. Are the bases and rates for allocating costs from each indirect pool consistently applied?

1048. Are the overhead pools formally and adequately

identified?

1049. What are the direct labor dollars and/or hours?

1050. What are the actual costs to date?

1051. Are the actual costs used for variance analysis reconcilable with data from the accounting system?

1052. At what point should variances be isolated and brought to the attention of the management?

1053. Are there knowledgeable Desktop Application projections of future performance?

1054. What is your organizations rationale for sharing expenses and services between business segments?

4.3 Earned Value Status: Desktop Application

1055. What is the unit of forecast value?

1056. Where is evidence-based earned value in your organization reported?

1057. If earned value management (EVM) is so good in determining the true status of a Desktop Application project and Desktop Application project its completion, why is it that hardly any one uses it in information systems related Desktop Application projects?

1058. When is it going to finish?

1059. How does this compare with other Desktop Application projects?

1060. How much is it going to cost by the finish?

1061. Are you hitting your Desktop Application projects targets?

1062. Earned value can be used in almost any Desktop Application project situation and in almost any Desktop Application project environment. it may be used on large Desktop Application projects, medium sized Desktop Application projects, tiny Desktop Application projects (in cut-down form), complex and simple Desktop Application projects and in any market sector. some people, of course, know all about earned value, they have used it for years - but perhaps not as effectively as they could have?

1063. Where are your problem areas?

1064. Validation is a process of ensuring that the developed system will actually achieve the stakeholders desired outcomes; Are you building the right product? What do you validate?

1065. Verification is a process of ensuring that the developed system satisfies the stakeholders agreements and specifications; Are you building the product right? What do you verify?

4.4 Risk Audit: Desktop Application

1066. Are team members trained in the use of the tools?

1067. Is the auditor able to evaluate contradictory evidence in an unbiased manner?

1068. Are auditors able to effectively apply more soft evidence found in the risk-assessment process with the results of more tangible audit evidence found through more substantive testing?

1069. What are risks and how do you manage them?

1070. Are audit program plans risk-adjusted?

1071. How do you govern assets?

1072. Are risk management strategies documented?

1073. Is risk an management agenda item?

1074. Do you have an understanding of insurance claims processes?

1075. Tradeoff: how much risk can be tolerated and still deliver the products where they need to be?

1076. Extending the consideration on the halo effect, to what extent are auditors able to build skepticism in evidence review?

1077. Does your board meet regularly and document

all decisions and actions?

1078. Is the number of people on the Desktop Application project team adequate to do the job?

1079. What effect would a better risk management program have had?

1080. Are regular safety inspections made of buildings, grounds and equipment?

1081. From an empirical perspective, does the business risk approach lead to a more effective audit, or simply to increased consulting revenue detrimental to audit rigor?

1082. How are risk appetites expressed?

1083. Do you record and file all audits?

1084. What limitations do auditors face in effectively applying risk-assessment results to the risk of material misstatement measures?

4.5 Contractor Status Report: Desktop Application

1085. Are there contractual transfer concerns?

1086. What is the average response time for answering a support call?

1087. What are the minimum and optimal bandwidth requirements for the proposed solution?

1088. How is risk transferred?

1089. What process manages the contracts?

1090. How long have you been using the services?

1091. Describe how often regular updates are made to the proposed solution. Are corresponding regular updates included in the standard maintenance plan?

1092. What was the actual budget or estimated cost for your organizations services?

1093. What was the final actual cost?

1094. What was the budget or estimated cost for your organizations services?

1095. If applicable; describe your standard schedule for new software version releases. Are new software version releases included in the standard maintenance plan?

1096. How does the proposed individual meet each requirement?

1097. What was the overall budget or estimated cost?

1098. Who can list a Desktop Application project as organization experience, your organization or a previous employee of your organization?

4.6 Formal Acceptance: Desktop Application

1099. Do you buy-in installation services?

1100. Was the Desktop Application project work done on time, within budget, and according to specification?

1101. Does it do what client said it would?

1102. General estimate of the costs and times to complete the Desktop Application project?

1103. Did the Desktop Application project manager and team act in a professional and ethical manner?

1104. Was the sponsor/customer satisfied?

1105. What features, practices, and processes proved to be strengths or weaknesses?

1106. Was business value realized?

1107. Who would use it?

1108. What can you do better next time?

1109. Was the client satisfied with the Desktop Application project results?

1110. Who supplies data?

1111. Have all comments been addressed?

1112. What lessons were learned about your Desktop Application project management methodology?

1113. Was the Desktop Application project goal achieved?

1114. What was done right?

1115. What is the Acceptance Management Process?

1116. What function(s) does it fill or meet?

1117. How does your team plan to obtain formal acceptance on your Desktop Application project?

1118. Did the Desktop Application project achieve its MOV?

5.0 Closing Process Group: Desktop Application

1119. How well defined and documented were the Desktop Application project management processes you chose to use?

1120. Can the lesson learned be replicated?

1121. What were the desired outcomes?

1122. What is the risk of failure to your organization?

1123. How critical is the Desktop Application project success to the success of your organization?

1124. Were sponsors and decision makers available when needed outside regularly scheduled meetings?

1125. Did the Desktop Application project management methodology work?

1126. Are there funding or time constraints?

1127. What is the amount of funding and what Desktop Application project phases are funded?

1128. What went well?

1129. What were things that you did very well and want to do the same again on the next Desktop Application project?

1130. What areas were overlooked on this Desktop Application project?

1131. What was learned?

1132. Mitigate. what will you do to minimize the impact should a risk event occur?

1133. Did you do what you said you were going to do?

1134. How well did the chosen processes produce the expected results?

1135. How will you know you did it?

5.1 Procurement Audit: Desktop Application

1136. Where funding is being arranged by borrowings, do corresponding have the necessary approval and legal authority?

1137. Has your organization taken a well-grounded decision about the procurement procedure chosen and has it documented the process?

1138. Are procurement processes well organized and documented?

1139. Were the specifications of the contract determined free from influence of particular interests of consultants, experts or other economic operators?

1140. Were the performance conditions under the contract comprehensive and unambiguous?

1141. Are buyers rotated so that they do not deal with the same vendors year in and year out?

1142. Are open purchase orders with a fixed monetary limitation used for local purchases of small dollar value?

1143. Is there an effective risk management system continuously monitoring procurement risk?

1144. Is the procurement process fully digitalized?

1145. Are fixed asset accounts posted currently?

1146. Were results of the award procedures published?

1147. Was suitability of candidates accurately assessed?

1148. Is there a forum where the departments suppliers performance is regularly considered with the suppliers?

1149. Are required quality and service standards set?

1150. Are information technology resources (e-procurement) used to reduce costs?

1151. Is there a legal authority for the procurement Desktop Application project?

1152. Are the right skills, experiences and competencies present in the acquisition workgroup and are the necessary outside specialists involved in part of the process?

1153. Was the estimation of contract value in accordance with the criteria fixed in the Directive?

1154. Has your organization examined in detail the definition of performance?

1155. Budget controls: does your organization maintain an up-to-date (approved) budget for all funded activities, and perform a comparison of that budget with actual expenditures for each budget category?

5.2 Contract Close-Out: Desktop Application

1156. Was the contract sufficiently clear so as not to result in numerous disputes and misunderstandings?

1157. Have all contracts been completed?

1158. Parties: Authorized?

1159. Have all contracts been closed?

1160. Have all acceptance criteria been met prior to final payment to contractors?

1161. How is the contracting office notified of the automatic contract close-out?

1162. Change in circumstances?

1163. Have all contract records been included in the Desktop Application project archives?

1164. What happens to the recipient of services?

1165. Parties: who is involved?

1166. What is capture management?

1167. Change in attitude or behavior?

1168. Was the contract type appropriate?

1169. Are the signers the authorized officials?

1170. Was the contract complete without requiring numerous changes and revisions?

1171. How/when used ?

1172. How does it work?

1173. Change in knowledge?

1174. Has each contract been audited to verify acceptance and delivery?

1175. Why Outsource?

5.3 Project or Phase Close-Out: Desktop Application

1176. What is the information level of detail required for each stakeholder?

1177. Have business partners been involved extensively, and what data was required for them?

1178. Who exerted influence that has positively affected or negatively impacted the Desktop Application project?

1179. Does the lesson describe a function that would be done differently the next time?

1180. How much influence did the stakeholder have over others?

1181. Who is responsible for award close-out?

1182. What hierarchical authority does the stakeholder have in your organization?

1183. What can you do better next time, and what specific actions can you take to improve?

1184. Were risks identified and mitigated?

1185. Is the lesson significant, valid, and applicable?

1186. Planned completion date?

1187. Planned remaining costs?

1188. What are the marketing communication needs for each stakeholder?

1189. What were the goals and objectives of the communications strategy for the Desktop Application project?

1190. What were the actual outcomes?

1191. Who are the Desktop Application project stakeholders and what are roles and involvement?

1192. What was the preferred delivery mechanism?

1193. What could be done to improve the process?

1194. What advantages do the an individual interview have over a group meeting, and vice-versa?

1195. Is the lesson based on actual Desktop Application project experience rather than on independent research?

5.4 Lessons Learned: Desktop Application

1196. What if anything has been lacking?

1197. Are there any hidden conflicts of interest?

1198. Are corrective actions needed?

1199. Did the team work well together?

1200. How accurately and timely was the Risk Management Log updated or reviewed?

1201. Were the Desktop Application project goals attained?

1202. How well do you feel the executives supported this Desktop Application project?

1203. What is the supervisor to staff ratio?

1204. What is the growth stage of your organization?

1205. Who has execution authority?

1206. What data are likely to be missing?

1207. What is your strategy for data collection?

1208. What should have been accomplished during predeployment that was not accomplished?

1209. Did the Desktop Application project management methodology work?

1210. How well is the build process working?

1211. How useful was your testing?

1212. How effective were Best Practices & Lessons Learned from prior Desktop Application projects utilized in this Desktop Application project?

1213. How useful and complete was the Desktop Application project document repository?

1214. How spontaneous are the communications?

Index

collected	32, 60-61, 63, 65, 70, 72, 169
collection	60, 187, 260
combine	85
coming	72
command	96
comments	251
commercial	153
commitment	99, 109
committed	67, 140, 155, 173, 201
committee	155-156, 207
common	131, 170, 173, 195, 210
community	171, 179
companies	1, 99, 224
company	7, 50, 65, 103, 105, 108, 112, 114, 119, 124
comparable	137
compare	70, 84, 244
compared	116, 176
comparing	75, 137
comparison	10, 190, 255
compatible	212, 222, 240
compelling	29
competing	53
competitor	242
compile	183
compilers	204
complaints	200
complete	1, 8, 10, 20, 35, 41, 156, 158-160, 162-163, 168-
170, 172, 185, 250, 257, 261	
completed	11, 28, 35, 37, 40, 131, 153, 163, 197, 228, 256
completely	171, 202
completing	114
completion	32, 37, 153, 163, 175, 182, 244, 258
complex	7, 107, 174, 244
complexity	18, 49
compliance	19, 48, 72, 83, 184, 235
complied	228
comply	131
component	225
components	149, 173, 194
compute	11
computer	150
concept	79
concern	56, 88, 232

preventive   205
prevents   24
previous   36, 173-174, 249
previously   138, 221
primary   47, 122, 130, 167
principles   136, 155, 194
priorities   46, 51-54, 181
priority 48-49, 159, 189
privacy   40, 138
problem   15, 17-20, 22-25, 27, 36-37, 39, 45-46, 65, 68, 217,
220, 245
problems   16-17, 22, 25, 87, 95, 120, 143, 185
procedure   153, 254
procedures   9, 77, 94, 98, 100, 139, 150, 153, 165, 170, 176,
184, 186-188, 194, 207, 231, 255
proceeding   171, 193
process   1-7, 9, 29, 31, 35-37, 41, 49, 59, 61-66, 68-71, 73,
89-92, 94-98, 100, 128, 135, 138, 142, 145, 147-149, 165, 169, 173,
184, 187, 201-203, 210, 212, 215, 224, 228-230, 233, 238, 245-246,
248, 251-252, 254-255, 259, 261
processes   31, 48, 50, 59-62, 64-65, 67, 71, 90, 93, 133, 136,
149, 188, 200, 208, 213, 215, 221, 231, 246, 250, 252-254
procuring   215
produce   63, 131, 136, 165, 218, 228, 253
produced   77, 239
producing   145
product   1, 44, 66, 70, 111, 119, 148, 181-182, 197, 204,
217-218, 229, 245
production   37, 75, 149, 231
productive   189
products   1, 17-18, 52, 105, 130, 135, 145, 153, 175, 216-217,
221, 240, 246
profession   197
profits 182
program   24, 56, 66, 95, 130, 136, 191, 199-200, 216, 238-
239, 246-247
programme   215, 239
programs   218, 226, 236
progress   28, 52, 84, 92, 110, 119, 150, 180, 188, 211, 215-
216, 232
prohibited   153

replicated   252
Report 5-6, 82, 95, 175, 200, 210, 217, 240, 248
reported   142, 210, 244
reporting   65, 95, 120, 139, 169, 183, 189, 200, 241
reports 90, 132, 156, 197, 207, 211, 220, 242
repository   156, 193, 208, 261
represent   182, 221
reproduced   1
reputation   107
request   5, 65, 181-182, 219, 221
requested   1, 76, 182, 209, 221
requests   220
require 38, 53, 68, 90, 93, 165, 174
required   18, 22, 29-30, 33, 36-37, 54, 72, 76, 82, 97, 129,
143, 157-160, 169, 172, 177, 187, 213, 231, 255, 258
requiring   132, 257
research   19, 111, 117, 133, 169, 225-226, 231, 259
resemble   215
Reserve   177
reserved   1
reserves   156, 175
reside 78
resolution   67, 85, 196
resolve 19, 22, 159, 228, 233
resolved   156, 174
resource   3-4, 123, 140, 155, 159, 165, 167, 193-194, 198,
217
resources   2, 7, 17, 19, 25, 35, 39, 42, 51, 60, 82, 94, 97, 113,
118, 123, 128, 133, 137, 148, 155, 157, 159-160, 164, 171, 179,
215, 229, 231, 237, 240, 255
respect   1
respond   135, 189, 199
responded   11
response   19, 24, 95-96, 197, 248
responses   86, 113, 199-200, 210, 227
responsive   179
restrict 143
result   61, 77, 148, 154, 179, 182, 186, 195, 221, 256
resulted   95
resulting   62, 147
results 8, 31-32, 70, 74, 78-79, 82-84, 87, 90-91, 136, 169, 180,
183, 185, 187, 215-216, 234, 246-247, 250, 253, 255
Retain 102

successful   71, 80, 96, 103, 107, 116, 131, 135, 167-168, 177,
213, 218, 236
succession   91
suddenly   198
sufficient   135, 210, 238-239
suggest   219
suggested   95, 182, 221
suitable   198, 204, 229
summary   242
supervisor   230, 235, 260
supplier   79, 107, 175, 225
suppliers   37, 59, 73, 117, 255
supplies   175, 250
supply 51, 161, 202
support   7, 25, 68, 90-91, 96, 108, 122-123, 165, 199, 201,
209, 213, 223, 226, 248
supported   72, 143, 201, 216, 260
supporters   134
supporting   82, 99, 187, 194
supportive   155, 192, 194
supports   234
surface   95
SUSTAIN   2, 75, 102
sustaining   94
symptom   15, 56
system 9, 65, 90, 117, 121, 142-144, 150, 167, 183, 190, 211, 222-
223, 225-227, 238, 243, 245, 254
systematic   55, 153
systems   62-63, 65, 70-71, 83, 87, 93, 133, 139, 207, 212,
225-226, 244
tackle 56
tactics 223-224
takers 147
taking 50, 135, 218, 231
talent 62, 120
talents 115
talking 7
tangible   246
target 41, 135, 156, 211, 213
targeted   211
targets 120, 129, 244
tasked 100
teaching   225